The Ultimate Game

Life

Do you know the rules?

David Innes Ritchie

Published by Wider Horizons

Foreword

© *David Ritchie 2007*

First published in Great Britain (2007) by Wider Horizons

This book is sold on the understanding that no part of it will be reproduced, resold, transmitted or circulated in any form other than that in which it is published without the publisher's prior consent

Contents

About the author vii
Acknowledgements ix
Foreword xi
Do you know the rules? 1
The Magic of the Universe 17
Going with the flow 61
Death, the Afterlife and Religion 79
Life and Abundance and Success 103
Relationships 123
Work and Business 151
The Future Happens Now 173
Playing the Game 199
Exercises 207
    Happiness 211
    Discipline 212
    Responsibility 214
    Focus and Concentration 217
    Know Thy Self 222
    Dreams 229
    Meditation 230
    Asking for help 235
    Setting the Scene 239
    Astral projection 239
    Healing 240
    Abundance 242
Notes 246

About the author

David Innes Ritchie

David is a forty something Scottish Born Entrepreneur, who has achieved significant commercial success both with Global Corporations and through starting and running a series of his own international businesses.

His passion for life and business, together with his charismatic approach, helps him meet challenges with enthusiasm and focus. As a visionary with the ability to think laterally, he has the experience and expertise necessary to spot opportunities, formulate winning solutions and then bring the necessary resources to bear in order to quickly make them a reality.

A gifted life and business coach, by nature he questions paradigms and has demonstrated that sound commercial expertise, allied to market understanding and technical competence consistently produces success.

He also shares a natural empathy with people, having risked and tackled most things first hand. His business highs and lows have been mirrored within his private life and his life long search for the answers to the questions we all share have culminated in the writing of this book.

David currently spends his time writing and pursuing his many business interests whilst travelling between California, Scotland and the Ukraine.

Acknowledgements

Wow this is a challenge as who do I miss out, so rather than think too much about it, I have decided to just let it flow. There are many that have helped shape me within the game of life, some deserve particular mention and others will just have to accept being named due to restricted space.

I'd like to thank my children Clare and Scott who were the catalyst for the book along with my Grandson Aidan. My mother May who just turned 69 as I write this and my father Bill who has passed over but is still with me, also my brothers Colin and Alan and Sister Lynn, my sister in law Jacqueline and brother in law Tibor, who I am enjoying getting to know all over again. My extended family, in particular my Uncle Robert and Uncle Bill, and Grandpa Grant, who were all larger than life for me as a child.

My loves which are fewer than most would suspect, Isobel, Cathy, Shona, JJ, Jax, Fay, and Irina. Cathy and Shona deserve a special mention as they both graced me by becoming my wife.

My friends and workmates, no doubt its been a challenge knowing me, Gary, George, Figgy, Steven, Tony O, Bill N, Bobby, Calum, Peter (Taz), Sean, Artie, Abdullah, Scott (Goalie), Craig, Jimbo, Gail, Michelle, Angela, David S, Catriona, Hayley, Laura, Scot (Hamish),The Hamil's, Cath, Pauline, Carol Ann and more recently, in this update, Tee, Paul, Tom and Dian, Eric (Big Luigi) and Lucy you all know how I feel about you.

There are many more that have touched me and you know who you are but lastly I want to thank JJ without who this would never have happened, Serge Pasquali for the artwork and for pushing JJ and John Ireland for the photography.

Foreword

Once upon a time, many years ago, on a magical beach in a small village called Findhorn, I met a young boy called David. I instantly recognised him, as he did me, but it was from another lifetime or maybe many life times before.

We were little more than children back then and together for a while during the summer we explored the mysteries and the magic of life and the Universe. We were happy, they were idyllic times. Then the inevitable happened. We both grew up and he went his way and I went mine until a quarter of a century later we found ourselves reunited again on that very same beach. This was no accident, this was destiny.

The first thing I noticed that day was the intensity and colour of his eyes, which were also filled with pain and anger and yet at the same time there was a kindness to them, a gentleness, that if you cared to look deeply enough, belied a deeply wounded soul. I later learned that few saw this because most were too scared to hold his gaze for long enough. He was, in a word, 'powerful'.

At that time he wanted to take his own life and I listened over the coming months as he poured out his thoughts and his feelings with brutal honesty, a rare thing indeed, and we talked and talked. I was deeply touched by the depth of his love for his wife, his family, his friends, and all who crossed his path, but most of all it was his truth that rocked me. He was broken but he was certainly not destroyed. Slowly, one step at a time, he started to take back his life.

There is little doubt that David is a charismatic character who has a profound effect on everyone he encounters. There are those who are terrified of him, jealous of him, those who admire him and look up to him, and there are those who love him for who he is, but there is no one, absolutely no one that isn't touched by his presence. We have known each other now for thousands of years and it is my belief that in this lifetime, we have finally settled a karmic debt.

David helped me to change my life. He was there for me through crisis and drama, all of my own doing of course, until the time came when I finally realised I would have to change my thinking. I did, and it was David that showed me how. His talent lay in giving step by step advice on what to do when facing a challenging situation.

I don't know where his wisdom came from, but I do know that when I followed his advice, for example, when selling my house, dealing with family issues, even falling in love again, everything fell into place in a way I could never have foreseen. I am not alone either. He has helped many people that I know of, and many others that I don't know personally.

I for one will be forever grateful to David for the love, compassion, and of course the advice that he has given unconditionally over the years. I am now delighted to see that he has finally written this book, which I believe has something in it for everyone.

One thing that always struck me was that when in David's presence, I had an overwhelming sense of higher powers at play but I never knew what it was or why. I felt compelled to write him a poem, which turned out to be in three different parts. I didn't realise it at the time and neither did he, but those poems were a message, a sign, they were not written by me, they were not intended for me, they came through me that's all. It is as if the three parts represented levels that David would have to go through on his journey before finally learning why he was here. It was only when he started to write this book that both of us realised the full significance of the message that lay between the words.

Perhaps there is a message for you in the words of this book. JJ.

Note from the author

The following poems were written a couple of years before I started to write the book, whilst they touched me at the time, the true significance only hit me when I was writing the final chapter of the book.

I decided to put Desire, Imagination, Creation and Experience in order and to my genuine surprise I found that it spelt DICE. Some may struggle to accept that something so obvious actually just dawned on me by accident, but as you will see when reading the book, there is no such thing as an accident.

I felt energised when the realisation set in and I took it as a sign that I was on the right track. I then remembered that JJ had used the word DICE in her poems and when I checked again, there it was in the final poem. I broke down and sobbed and as the tears streamed down my face, something very deep shifted inside me. It was a truly enlightening moment and I called JJ from California to share this insight with her.

Genesis

In the beginning there was light
And he came to me on a whim
With such toil and trouble
Bubbling within
He was witty and wise, had no secrets to keep
With a magical mind
Lost in the deep dark world of imaginings
He built empires from thoughts
And tore them down - again and again
Appeasing his anger but igniting his pain
And each time as he took the blame
He burned
He sought solace in beauty and love
In passionate pleasures
And desperate flirtations
So empty, dishonest
I could feel his brilliance
And his light
As he struggled to shine
In such a hostile world
For his delicate mind
But everyone knew
He was one of a kind
And he touched my soul
With his truth
This man that I met in my youth
As he breathed fire into pain
In order to live again
And I could only listen
In admiration
As he questioned without hesitation
His fears his hopes and his life
His longings, his needs,
And his wife
And he grew and I knew
He knew it too

Awakenings

Beating drums, shaman dreams,
Animal powers and flowing streams
Meditation, casting stones
Candlelight and great unknowns
Breathing, dreaming, probing deep
Tranquil moments, restless sleep
Fear and terror, pain and sorrow
Hanging on until tomorrow…
As he cries
No more lies
Please
And I heard not his words
But his wisdom
As he blew me away with his mind
In solitary contemplations
And momentary hesitations
He let go of expectations
Only to find
That he weeps on the inside
Whilst others play the game
And all in his name
On the outside
So I hold him from a distance
Both night and day
As he learns
That nature
Does it her way

Enlightenment

He's a powerful man, a man of vision
Yet he knows not his own strength
He could light the darkest of paths
With his fiery intent
His passions are fierce,
His longings more so
And his search for peace
Seems painfully slow
Yet his mission is only just beginning
Although its roots lie in another lifetime
Like the greatest thinkers long gone before
He has a secret knowledge
You cannot learn in school or college
There is no map
No well trodden path
Just the wandering soul
That chooses to follow
Truth
This much he knows, and when he outgrows
His outer protections
His inner reflections will outshine
All others
For he is one of a special kind
Chosen to break the spells that bind
Darkness to light
And though he pays the higher price
As he takes his turn and casts the dice
He will find...
Contentment
Priceless beyond any measure
And peace of mind
The real treasure of enlightenment

It doesn't matter how you tell

the truth, the truth will

always tell itself

Do you know the rules?

"The reality is that we all instinctively know and feel the truth but if we remain closed and unaware, we allow our pre-programmed responses and the chattering of our minds to trick us into believing illusions"

Now why would anyone want to call something as important and as precious as life itself a Game?

Well! Isn't life meant to be fun and joyous? Why should it be miserable? In fact, as you will see from reading on, the only way to get the very best from life and to create all that you desire, is by lightening up, lifting your spirit, increasing your vibration, and learning how to really play the game. If you can do this you can become Truly Rich and enjoy abundance in everything that life has to offer.

I have used the analogy of a game as this is far more palatable and acceptable than speaking in religious or psychological terms. We all understand the concept of a game, and inevitably, there are basic rules to follow in order to get the best out of any game.

In this case the game is the ultimate game, the game of life itself. Anyway, I liked the title and it is how I have chosen to look at this journey we all call life.

Setting the scene

When reading this book I would strongly recommend that you find your own special place to read it, whatever works for you. I read today that someone found that airport lounges were the best place for them.

If possible, light a candle or burn some incense, just do whatever you can to show that you are being receptive and open, not just to what I have to say, but more importantly, to any thoughts and ideas that may be triggered within you.

Feel the words and take time over them as there is a message in just about every paragraph. Please read the whole book from start to finish as it flows and tells a story and the temptation to jump to a chapter that you think is of particular interest may only serve to confuse you as you will not have learned the how and the why that has gone before. Most of all enjoy reading it and all that it might spark inside your being.

I am very fortunate in that my lifestyle exposes me to all sorts of people and cultures and invariably I choose to share snippets of my understanding of life with those I meet along the way.

I have yet to come across anyone who not only listens intently but validates their own agreement and understanding by sharing their own personal experiences and stories with me. This is refreshing, especially when it comes from those who you least expect it from and this encourages me to continue to share.

So, I am about to share with you my interpretation of the game in the simplest, clearest, purest way that I can. In all that I write there will be practical, psychological, and spiritual elements so everyone should be able to find something that they can connect to or resonate with.

I have written this as I said before, first and foremost for my children, as I would like them to understand what I have come to understand and to provide them with choices.

Secondly, I realise that I have also written it for all those that I love and who love me.

Thirdly, I dedicate it to the entire human race, past, present and future, and to anything and everything else in the Universe, visible or not, as we are all participating in the game, as you will see.

If you are feeling slightly bemused, or concerned by the use of certain language, relax. I assure you it will all become clear as you read on.

Will I be endorsing certain statements in the book by saying that as so many million believe this it must be true? No I will most certainly not. This is unashamedly my own personal offering given freely to you to do with it what you will as we all have freedom of choice.

I have trusted my intuition, what feels right, and what ultimately makes sense to me, whilst at the same time remaining open to all possibilities and guidance from whatever source, and as far as I am aware, I have remained non-judgemental as I write.

This is therefore *my* interpretation of the truth and if any of it resonates with you, or feels right to you too, then I will have added some value to the experience of life.

The reality is that we all instinctively know and feel the truth but if we remain closed and unaware, we allow our pre-programmed responses and the chattering of our minds to trick us into believing illusions and staying within our comfort zones, which is a horrible, stagnant place to be.

Hopefully soon you will be able to break free of these invisible chains and look forward to creating your very own personal adventure through the ultimate game, the only real game, the game of LIFE

Tame the ego

My son Scott, despite his youth (he is 20 years old), has chosen his path, a life in the entertainment industry, and was recently in a tribute boy band working his way towards his goal. He is now in the final stages of securing a record deal.

Scott has inspired me greatly, and I listen intently, sometimes to be honest with a loving element of surprise to the words of wisdom that both he and his sister Clare (she is 22 years old) often share with me. They both make me so proud and regularly evoke in me tears of joy as they touch my soul. Clare with her constant heartfelt communications oozing with love and affection and Scott with whom I have the added luxury of being able to listen to whenever I want just by playing his music, and that same love and emotion is clearly expressed in all that he sings.

It is my intention to make them as proud of me as I am of them and therefore all that I do here in this book is dedicated to them in the first instance.

Scott has recently spent a period of time on the Spanish island of Majorca learning his trade and stage skills by doing practical performances. Before leaving for Spain, he entered a singing competition, more for something to do rather than a conscious desire to compete, and my advice to him was not to try and show how technically competent he was, but to do what he was meant to do, to entertain. He did, and he won. Likewise with me, I have no intention of trying to show you how clever or right I am in the words of this book. So why do I mention all this?

I mention it because I want to stimulate your mind, sow some seeds, show you why it is so important to **tame your ego** and nurture clean and pure thoughts.

For clarity, ego can be insecurity driven as well as over confidence. Ironically, each normally leads to the opposite effect. Insecurity makes you try too hard and being over confident means you don't try hard enough.

Ultimately, my intention is to make you happy, to stimulate you, to help you become aware and open and just like Scott, I also hope to entertain you along the way too as all games should be fun to play.

Learn how to play – believe in the magic

The chains of fear are habit forming and at first they are so light that you are barely aware of them, it is only when they have grown heavy through habit that you feel they are impossible to break. Yes they are difficult, but impossible? NO! What I will share with you will help, that I can promise you.

The reason I am being bold and stating that it is *my truth*, sharing it with you as I do and taking full responsibility for my thoughts and comments, is because I have demonstrated to those that know me well, that I already knew most of the answers to the questions discussed in so many well written books on the subject, without ever having read them. Does this make me special?

Not at all, I am just tuned in and aware of an ability that we all share. Where does this knowledge come from? Well, that's all part of the book. Some might call it magic, and I must admit I love that word, and in a sense it is, as life is magical once you learn how to play and accept and embrace the rules of the game.

We can all be magicians and shape a truly fantastic Universe in which to play, learn, and grow, because once tuned in, you understand that learning and growing is what life is all about.

Children are born believing in magic, it is naturally interwoven into their play. They are already tuned in when they arrive on this plane but unfortunately, we quickly encourage them to tune out.

They are no sooner here and we start to teach them a depressing game built around FEAR, WANT, LOSS, WORK, STRESS, VIOLENCE, MISERY, GREED, and DECEPTION, and so on, and so on. We may *think* we are doing the best for them by encouraging them to get serious about life, to fear just about everything and to trust no one, but are we?

Try to remember the last time you allowed yourself to play as freely and as uninhibited as a child and you will get an insight into the magic that can be released when you remember the rules to the original game of life and the reason you are here on earth today, the magic you have very nearly lost. I say very nearly because it isn't lost, it is just hidden from those who choose not to feel and not to see.

So if you like, I am planting the seed within you so that you are equipped to play the game to the best of your ability. Once planted, this seed will grow and blossom and provide you with an abundance of fruit to sustain you.

How fast it grows will depend on how well you care for it and nurture it within. To make it a bit easier, I will provide you with the basic rules of the game, but the ultimate path you take is very much up to you.

Find your path and join in

A close friend of mine I call JJ, whom I love dearly and who first actively demonstrated the mostly forgotten gift of magic to me when I was a teenager, encouraged me to embark on this journey into the world of words and wisdom.

I used to joke *hey I'm an engineer not a bloody poet* besides my grammar is atrocious. Ironically, I was proud of my attempts at poetry and the power within the words, but sadly for me like many others, my poems were nearly always generated during periods of inner turmoil and darkness, rarely inspired by joy and contentment.

Thankfully those days are now firmly in the past and here I am writing a book that in the darkest recesses of my mind I always knew I'd have to write, I had merely forgotten why I was here.

Back to the point, JJ reckons I have an astute ability to give step by step advice so that's what I'm going to do. At the same time I will attempt to explain why things work as there is a power in knowing. In other words, to achieve whatever, first you must do this, and then you must do that, and this is why.

The natural flow of which direction to take in any scenario all becomes very obvious to me when I combine my own personal life experiences (and believe me, I've had a few) with intuition, an innate inner sense or innocence we all have and can develop, and which can be considered one of your greatest gifts.

I will also share what happens when you don't go with the flow, as I have been that muppet many, many times before. Hopefully you will be able to glean something from the pain of my attempts at swimming against the flow rather than risk battering yourself on rocks, or worse, drowning in a sea of misery.

I have been writing the outline to this book in my head for many years, a lifetime or more, so why am I doing it now right at this moment?

Well I have learned the basic rules of the game, however I'm still learning how to play it well and that is an important point to emphasise. I am still learning, and like all games, I need to keep practicing and the referee in the game (karma) still has to caution me from time to time.

It all seems so very clear to me that if I share this information about the nature of the Universe and invite you all to join me, not only will I have playmates in the game (I have spent many years playing solitaire and feeling isolated) it will rapidly change all our lives for the better.

Also as a result of my desire I now have the creativity and the energy to reactivate and drive my imagination. I also have the time. Well actually I always had the time in the sense that time is the one thing that we all have in common, we all have the same 24 hours in a day, and it is how we use these hours that separates and defines us.

Live in the NOW

There are many things we all have in common which should come as no surprise as we are all connected and are all part of the same whole, but sticking with the subject of time for a moment…

I once met a Funeral Director in a social situation. He was in fact visiting a friend of mine, a guy called Neil, a colourful character, as all my friends tend to be. Neil was and still is the owner of the local water ski centre where I lived at the time in Loch Earnhead in Scotland. Sadly, I cannot recall the funeral director's name but it was his words that blew me away.

He arrived riding one of the latest Ducati sports motorbikes, and appeared to be one of the happiest guys I had ever encountered. Both the bike and the joyful demeanour may seem at odds with an image of a funeral director, and it certainly seemed strange to me at the time, but he shared with me something that afternoon and his words have stuck with me ever since.

"*Imagine you were born wearing a watch that ticked backwards to the time of your death showing the time you have left in this life. I guarantee that you would lead your life very differently and not waste a second*".

Think about that for a moment and ask yourself if you would do things differently. The chances are you most certainly would. Put simply, it is important to learn to live in the NOW, one of the main rules in the game.

Interestingly, whilst the practice of meditation brings with it many benefits, one of the key things that I obtained from it was learning to take the time for me, to actually meditate, to place that stop on everything else and take time to re-adjust and put things back into perspective, to remind myself that all I have is now. So it's not just the act of meditation itself but the self-discipline and the courage to make it happen and to take the time to do it.

Self-discipline

I would love to say that as soon as I heard the message from the funeral director, I immediately started to live in the NOW, but no, I did not. It was some time later that I learned how to put it into practice and I'm still practicing.

It struck me and had a huge impact on me at the time, but like many things, if you don't discipline yourself and have a clear sense of direction and purpose and understand why you are doing whatever it is you are doing then good intentions can quickly pass and fade.

So discipline is another important key element of the game along with focus and knowing in which direction you want to go. Think of any game or sport. If you want to be really good at it what do you need to do?

First of all you have to love playing whatever game or sport it is and you have to have the desire. Then you need to practice it and practice it until you get it as finely tuned as possible, until it becomes second nature, and this is where discipline comes in.

You also need to know what you are trying to achieve and what the end result will be. Do you think that world's greatest sportsmen and sportswomen roll over and go back to sleep in the morning? They may well want to, but their desire to perfect their game is greater.

The game of life is no different. If you are disciplined and do the exercises until they become habitual and intuitive, you will no longer have to think about it at all, you will just do it, naturally.

Avoid the rocks

In my life so far I have experienced a number of lessons, come up against many obstacles I needed to face, and hit quite a few rocks pretty hard whilst going against the flow. I have cried in the depths of despair, I've gone to extremes in my relationships, been married and divorced twice, experienced bankruptcy, battled with suicidal thoughts, and a few years ago, my father committed suicide. These are just a few examples but collectively, they shook me into action and thankfully, I am now happier and more contented than I have ever been.

It has to be said that on my travels along the rocky river of life I have also had great success. I have had the opportunity to play on a global playground and experience different cultures as my business interests have taken me overseas, but most importantly, I am now able to live the life I want to live.

The reason I feel compelled to share my experience, my joy and my understanding with each of you in any way that I can, is because maybe, just maybe, it will stop some of you from hitting the same rocks as I did, it's so unnecessarily painful and trust me, your focus and energy are better spent elsewhere.

Learn from others

I recently discovered Warren Buffett, supposedly the second richest man in the world. What I mean by that is that I had heard about him, but knew very little about the man. I stumbled across an interview he had given and I immediately warmed to him on many levels, some of which I will share as we go along.

He joked that it was far better to learn from other people's mistakes, especially his, than to repeat them yourself. He used an interesting anecdote but to put it simply, he suggested that you look at people you admire and copy what you admire and at the same time look at aspects of people whom you don't like and eliminate those aspects from your own life.

He, for me, epitomises certain aspects of the game as he recently donated the majority of his fortune to charity and lives his life very modestly in comparison to his wealth in monetary terms. It would appear that he recognises the difference between need and want and knows how to put things in perspective. Admittedly, I have only glanced at the surface of his life and can't help but wonder if he, like me, has at times missed out on some aspects of life when focussing more on trying to conclude a deal than anything else. Regardless, I found myself drawn to this humble and humorous character and will research his life further as a matter of interest.

Getting back to the point of learning from others, there are plenty of people, books and examples that we can choose to follow in order to change and become what we want to be, but sadly, few of us ever do. Why? What is it that stops the majority of people from taking that next step?

Read on and discover how the Universe works and learn how to stimulate your desire and find the strength to break those debilitating and restrictive chains of fear that hold you back.

Freedom of choice

I recently wrote to someone that I care for very much and who at the time was very troubled and mixed up. Her desire was to retreat and to be left alone and so I had to respect this. I wouldn't have in the past and instead would have tried to force a solution on her. At the same time, I wanted so much to be able to help her. She was afraid and like most people who are scared, she was confused. It's all part and parcel of the same thing.

I told her that I would always be her lighthouse so that on clear days she would be able to see me from afar, a symbol of strength and safety to return to, and on the dark and stormy days, I would be there to act as her light, to show her the way, so she could avoid the rocks, if she chose to do so.

The key point here is if she chose to do so. I reiterate this as it's a very important point which is that each and every one of us has freedom of choice to choose our own path. We should never ever try to manipulate someone else's will, or force them to act or behave in a certain way because it's what we want or believe is best for them. We have to allow them to go their own way, no matter how bizarre a route that might seem to you.

The only thing you can do is be there for them if they hit the rocks, or act as a guiding light to show them a way through if they find themselves in troubled waters. So all I could do was choose to reassure her and deal with my own longing and pain at her suffering. This is putting the rules of the game into practice.

Once again, this is a very personal book and everything you read here is my own opinion based on my own life experiences to date. It will either strike a chord with you or not. I hope it does.

They say that when you are ready to be taught, the teacher will appear. One would hope that given the fact that you are reading this at all means you are at least open to possibility.

I am also going to purposely avoid labouring a point. I personally love books that get to the crux of the matter and that don't spend pages and pages telling you over and over again what you accepted quite readily in the first few paragraphs.

There are plenty of books out there that cover each and every topic discussed in this book and in much greater detail than here so if you so desire, go search them out.

Reading on you may disagree with everything I have to say, or you might feel compelled to do your own research and validate your own truth, or perhaps you will think "WOW! This feels so right". Whatever your reaction or your point of view, in each and every case I would ask you to look deep inside yourself for that little flame that burns within us all, the flame of life. Do you need to rekindle yours?

Do you wish to re engage in the game of life or perhaps play the game better? If yes, you need to know the rules?

It doesn't matter how you tell the truth, the truth will always tell itself.

Playing in the Light

I am reminded of a story that I have heard many variations of the crux of which is that there are some people who have spent their lives chained up and facing a wall in a dark cave. Behind them they hear people going about their business and can feel the warmth of a fire that also casts shadows onto their wall. For them this is their reality, this is their life.

One day one of them decides that he wishes to turn and face the warmth and the light and making a huge effort he discovers that the chains are not locked but are loosely bound just like the chains of fear created by habit. He tries to tell the others but no one listens and even if they believed him, most would not be prepared to take the risk.

Drawn to the light he moves away, only to be blinded by that very same light. Slowly but surely as his eyes become accustomed he drinks in the wonders that he sees, wonders that those already living in the light take for granted. As time passes, he begins to miss his companions in the cave so he returns to try and persuade them to join him in the light so that they too can experience the beauty that he has seen. They think he is mad. Reluctantly he decides to stay in the cave and settles down to face the wall. However, he cannot stay, it all seems so meaningless and empty because once you have seen the light, you can never return to the dark.

The ultimate game is all about seeing the wonders that you have taken for granted, showing you how you can positively resist and in turn create light in your everyday life.

How long have you been playing the game in the dark unable to see the rules or the wonders that lie before you?

Let there be light…

The Magic of the Universe

"So whilst we can and do affect our bodies by what we eat and how we act, the biggest impact is created by what we think"

What is you inner voice saying?

Let us begin, by setting the scene and the objective.

Life is truly magical. In fact, we are all magicians, creators, and as a result we are all capable of getting everything that we desire from life and much, much more.

This is actually more straightforward to achieve than what you might think, with the results being in direct proportion to your level of desire, how faithful you are to your cause, how disciplined and how grateful and how open to receiving everything that you are.

Seems pretty simple when we put it like that and it is certainly easy to say, but I can hear all the excuses and justifications being voiced as to why it might not relate to you. Stop just for a minute and listen. What is your inner voice saying?

Is it *no way* or *maybe* or *but*? Or is it saying *yes, tell me more*? Take note of what your inner voice is saying to you as that will let you see where your own barriers are and there is a certain power in recognising and knowing what is going on inside your mind at a deep level.

Alchemy is not the magic of changing base metals into gold but it is about transforming your existence into what you truly desire. In other words you can and do shape your own reality.

My intention is that by bringing to your awareness how everything works, and by embracing and understanding your truth, the absolute truth and the rules of the Universe, you can start to eliminate debilitating and restricting fears.

Learn emotional control

I believe that what I am about to share are natural laws that have always been in existence and are not and should not be perceived to be in conflict with any original religious teachings. In fact if looked at with an open mind it will give you a deeper understanding of your world and enhance your chosen religion whether that is spiritually based, scientific or practical. So let us proceed.

Few would argue that at any level this is a truly amazing Universe that we live in. The advent of television, movies, and the internet, are simple examples that most of us will easily relate to and so a good starting point on our journey of discovery. They are criticised by some because of the garbage sometimes produced, and also because some people become addicted and dependent on them and start to just exist as a result rather than lead full and active lives.

Sadly, these people do not see them for what they are – man made tools, but they are still potentially very useful man made tools, provided it is accepted that they are just that, just another tool in the tool box, or an accessory to the game.

Digressing for a moment, I use the term *addicted* purposely, as TV is probably one of the most widely consumed drugs that currently exists in the world today, followed closely by the Internet and virtual games. So! Should they be banned carte blanche?

No! Banning anything is a form of weakness and an admission of failure or lack of control and there is a definite place and role in life for resistance.

Yes, for many, abstinence is best or possibly the only way to control their emotional dependence but outright banning is wrong.

Everything has a place and as you will see, learning emotional control is the key to it all. TV and other forms of medium are not evil in themselves, just like money isn't evil, they are simply man made and therefore the emotional aspect is placed on them by man. Rather than being evil, it is the misplaced love or need of them that is the real issue.

Taking responsibility

Another point worthy of reflection is that if we consider accepting that TV is a drug or the effective delivery of a drug by way of content, then ultimately, who are the drug dealers and what are their primary objectives?

Is it merely entertainment or is that just a disguise for helping to control and dumb down the masses? Regardless it is clear that there is something missing and a need that is not being met, otherwise it would not have the impact that it has.

Dramatic, thought provoking and controversial stuff worthy of debate, however putting such statements aside and focussing on the positive, the TV could be used for so much good but we all have to take responsibility for it and choose what we want it to be used for and to act on that. Is the drug being issued and dispersed responsibly?

I was watching an interview with Al Gore where he was being asked if he would consider running for president again. He acknowledged that he wanted to have an impact on the world and that possibly the best chance he had of doing this would be as the President of the United States of America as no other position appeared to have as much power.

However, he also struggled with aspects of politics today, the media dynamic being one such aspect. Why is there so much time being dedicated to the affairs of the likes of the Paris Hiltons and Britney Spears of this world rather than the really important issues in life.

Like all drugs, TV acts as a means of escape and whilst some reality pills may be unpalatable and difficult to swallow, it is in our best interests to know the truth so the reality MUST also be shown and shared. Ironically, in doing so, the moments of escape would seem all the sweeter so there would be a win-win situation.

Currently, what limited *reality bites* there are, are lost amongst a sea of trivia and the current ongoing intention appears to be yet more trivia and sensationalism. Once again, it's up to us to choose, just as it is our choice as to what food stuffs and drinks we choose to consume.

Just for the moment we will put aside the positive and enlightening content that thankfully does exist and is shown within these communication mediums, and which would otherwise not be exposed or shared with the world *en masse* if those mediums did not exist.

The message

Let us imagine someone from an isolated tribe being exposed to television, a movie or the internet for the very first time. They would most likely think it truly magical, and would see it for the wonders that it contained, and would no doubt be spellbound and would listen and believe every word that was emitted as a result, hence the reason that some responsibility needs to be exercised with regard to content.

If you had never been exposed to this type of technology before, or if you were unaware, or not tuned in, you might even mistake some of the rubbish coming through these mediums for the truth.

You would find it difficult to differentiate between what was true and what was not. The radio broadcast The War of the Worlds by Orson Wells being a prime example. Or, we could use the example of the cargo cult stories.

A certain tribe of natives (the name escapes me at the moment) during World War 2 saw planes landing on runways, and they saw that these planes were bringing food and other essential supplies to the people there. These natives believed that all they had to do was to replicate the same thing and the planes would bring cargo to them too. So, they built runways and watchtowers, and even constructed makeshift headphones and marched in a similar fashion to the soldiers.

Yet we in the so called civilised world not only take technology for granted, we in fact expect and demand more and more from communication mediums. On one level this is healthy as all creation, growth and positive change is good and necessary. But more importantly we also take the content for granted, because of the deluge of trivia, we have become conditioned to treating it as purely visual entertainment, and sometimes even just a background blur or noise and rarely do we try and empathise or look for the message or the wonder within. This needs to change.

Awareness

I am a natural empathiser and can become highly emotional watching a film or a programme on TV, much to my kids and loved ones embarrassment. I cry openly with tears of joy or sadness, even on the plane, as I always seem to get or see a message somewhere.

Perhaps this book will help you become more aware, more in tune, just be open to the possibility. It is no accident (there are no accidents) that there have been an increasing number of enlightened movies and programs being produced, mostly wrapped up in an entertainment package, just like a sugar coated pill for kids because it's easier to swallow, easier to accept.

Unfortunately this, like the sugar on the pill, can mask the intent and although it can and will impact on you subconsciously, what we want is to bring things into your conscious awareness so that you know why things happen and why you behave in a certain way.

Regardless, getting back to the point, the good that does exist all helps expose the wonders of the Universe and the magic that lies behind it. As I said this is no accident and helps fuel the growing awareness and acceptance that there is a magic (magic is merely science we don't yet fully understand) at work and makes the acceptance of new things more palatable whether you are consciously aware of it or not.

Our recent generations have witnessed science fiction becoming fact in their own lifetimes and there is so much more being created than what we are exposed to in our daily lives as generally, we are only fed what is commercially viable whether it is good for us or not.

In our world today, money always seems to be the deciding factor. There are countless developments that we are never exposed to but they exist nonetheless. For example, the former Soviet Union is awash with sophisticated inventions as they, on the whole, were less commercially driven, but they have never been shared globally or even nationally, as there was no commercial aspect. The positive in all this is that if we take the time to reflect on it then it may just stimulate us to see that dreams and what we may have deemed to be pure fantasy can in fact become a reality.

Everything has a place, a role, in life or the Universe, and I am reminded of the words of a former business partner of mine, Abdullah El Maazi, who whilst Arab by birth, spoke the Queen's English with no detectable accent whatsoever and he was fluent in a number of languages. I admired his wisdom. Sadly, we had a disagreement and we drifted apart and lost touch, which I deeply regret, as I miss him.

One day when we were together, I commented on the number of papers he read each day and he replied *one day soon David, doing what you do in this international business that we have together, you will pick up the paper and everything will have a relevance and a connection and you too will wish to know what is happening in the world, the world we all share.*

His words proved to be true, everything does have a connection. Just like the concept of a butterfly flapping its wings on one side of the globe and a hurricane taking place on the other. Likewise once you grasp all that is written here, and of course the rules of the game, you will see the messages and connections everywhere, and I am sure things will just pop into your head from a movie or program and you will say *ah! Now I understand.*

The reason I have mentioned television, movies and the internet rather than books at this juncture, is that books are very personal things that rely more on your imagination, unless you are being read a story. However through these other mediums the masses are exposed to information in a very different manner than books, relying less on imagination as the pictures are painted for you so you either accept what you see or you don't.

This in no way lessens the importance of books, as they have their own particular magic as you can paint your own pictures based on your interpretation and terms of reference, and I for one love reading.

Are we superior?

So, getting back to the point of mass communication, we can if we choose, access a daily reminder of the wonders and miracles of the magic of the Universe through these mediums. Just watch any nature documentary and look at the vast array of incredible species that exist, many if not all with abilities that we cannot match or even come close to, and yet we love to feel superior.

Every day new discoveries of life and creatures are exposed, often existing where it was once thought impossible to live and where we certainly could not, such as deep in rock and miles below the sea, where the pressure would crush our skulls far less our lungs and in temperatures beyond our limits, and without even light or oxygen.

I could go on and on listing things, and no doubt many are springing into your mind as you read, and still we actually feel superior. We have fascinating documentaries about ancient civilisations, some all but wiped out and their messages apparently lost. Once again on examination most seemed advanced to a level way beyond what we believe could have been possible at that time.

It is fascinating that the ancient Egyptians all those thousands of years ago worshipped a star that we only discovered a few decades ago with the latest telescopes, Sirius B.

The Mayan calendar was incredibly accurate and they were even able to pinpoint the age of the known universe, something we have only recently got close to. They also built structures that we struggle to comprehend even today, despite what we assume is our leading edge technology and equipment.

We of course find it difficult to truly contemplate what it would be like thousands of years ago as many cannot even recall what it was like without central heating or air-conditioning.

Equally intriguing is the fact that similar statues, carvings and structures can be found all over the world that existed in parallel time with each other, with man at the time having no obvious ability to cover the distances involved or any obvious way of communicating, and yet each of these far reaching, dispersed cultures, also all share similar fables and stories, such as their own versions of the biblical Noah's Ark, which features in at least 200 different ancient religions across the world.

We as man destroyed or buried or hid most of this away each time we conquered or allegedly civilised a people, and yet we still feel superior.

The Universe is equally fascinating looking outward rather than inward. Many years ago I was asked to go to the Edinburgh Astronomy centre where they had at that time one of two digital devices that cost in the millions and which were used to map the known Universe. They also provided assistance to guide the Hubble telescope.

I was asked if I could come up with additional commercial uses for this equipment that could see so many thousand shades of colour and detail. I did, but never got a chance to share them, however, whilst involved I was aghast at the size and scale of the known observable Universe.

The digitrometer used photographic plates and there were approx 400,000 planets on each plate, and 12,000 plates, therefore running into the billions, meaning that we are one tiny planet amongst millions of others, and yet we still think we are superior.

I could go on and on with example after example of the wonders and magic of the Universe but I think you get the point, that the Universe is vast and no matter where we look in it we can find magic and wonder, and hopefully I have stimulated your mind. I will deal with some specific aspects later in more detail.

So it takes little imagination to see that we take so much for granted and this raises serious questions. Do we have much to learn? Or more importantly, have we forgotten a great deal? Or are we shielded from the truth?

I repeated a few times above the fact that we feel superior. We love to think of ourselves as being somehow more special than anything else, but are we superior? I would say given the evidence, it would at first glance appear not. On the surface we seem to be good at destruction and killing and have destroyed and made extinct more species than any natural disaster. Some schools of thought believe the demise of the woolly mammoth and other extinct creatures was a result of man. Sadly, in fact scarily over a $1/3^{rd}$ of the worlds species have become extinct in the last 50 years due to the impact of so called civilised man.

Perhaps a virus that kills us could be classed as superior to us but do you feel inferior to a virus? I suppose you would if it was killing you. The answer is you still feel superior, and regardless of what I said above, you feel that way deep down and on one level you are partly justified, as we do have certain superior abilities. Or is it better to say that we have abilities that differentiate us as the word superior does have negative connotations attached to it, for me anyway.

What differentiates us from other life forms?

So what is it that *we* have that other species appear not to have and which differentiates us from other life forms? We can decide later whether we have used this gift properly, abused it, or just become down right lazy. The good news is that we all have this ability. *What is it?* I hear you say. Relax I have not even scratched the surface of the magic of the Universe yet. But, ok so how do we differ?

Some may immediately think its consciousness versus instinct and yes without conscious awareness as a starting point we would be truly robotic and merely exist. Instinct implies a lack of thought and again could be thought of as robotic, however and it is a BIG HOWEVER which will be covered later in more depth there is a significant difference between mechanical programmed thought and freedom of thought that taps into a universal consciousness or memory bank. So whilst animals or other species may seem to act purely instinctively this need not mean robotic or lack of consciousness.

Fortunately like everything in the Universe I can put it to you very simply. What differentiates us is **Desire and Imagination**. The thing that all human beings share is desire. We would not move a single muscle to do anything if it was not first fuelled or driven by desire. Fact! Think about it, what drives your every action?

We also differ from everything else because of imagination, an incredibly powerful tool that we all possess but generally use less and less effectively as we get older. Imagination takes the thought initiated by desire and shapes it so that it starts to become a reality and it is as simple and straightforward as that.

That alone is what gives us our so called superiority and that's where we differ from just about everything else, the fact that we have desire and imagination.

Let me give you a very simple taster of the power it can tap into and that we can all relate to, however, it is obviously much, much more than this. In fact it shapes you, your reality, and the Universe, but this is just a starter on a level that everyone should be able to grasp, especially as it relates to sex which is always an attention grabber.

A guy is lazing on the couch feeling shattered and lifeless and just as he is about to drift off to sleep, he catches a glimpse of a women undressing in the next door building. His attention is roused

The Magic of the Universe

and his desire activated and his imagination goes into overdrive. He is suddenly alert and full of energy. Where did that energy come from? Was it magic? Did he plug himself in?

Well in fact he did, to a hidden reserve within, and in turn, a universal truth. I will expand and clarify this later but first you will be saying that there has to be more to it all than this, and yes, if you wish to complicate matters there is, and hence there are a number of chapters in this book, but on a simple level here is the basic rule.

Desire leads to thought, the imagination shapes this and desire kicks in again and causes us to act, and in the whole scheme of things that's it, we can create our own reality and have whatever we desire.

Let us be clear and separate very distinctly the difference between need and desire or need and want. This is important as our uncontrolled desires or wants has led us to accumulate more than what we need and single-handedly has led to the majority of the planet's issues we have to deal with today. No other species takes or kills more than what it needs to survive. More on this later.

AH! But this ability only happens for some special magical few you say, or it's just a big cosmic joke or illusion.

Yes some do seem or appear to be more blessed than others but the reality is we all can and I will show you how. Also keep firmly in mind that appearances can be deceptive so those that you envy may very well be envying you.

I personally have had many experiences of this whereby I have admired someone greatly only to discover later on that they admired me too and yet many years passed and we never shared this truth with each other, on reflection, I see this is such a waste.

Why do we have this gift, this ability, and what is the purpose of it? Why are we here and what's it all about?

The purpose of our existence is to use this ability to experience, learn and grow, and here is the cosmic joke and the irony of it all. Brace yourself. The happier you are and the lighter your spirit, then the easier it is to achieve your objective or your heart's desire.

Please note that there is no mention of work or sacrifice, skills, talent and so on. Yes, the happier you are the lighter your spirit, the easier it is and there is a reason why this works as will become clear to you as you read on.

Unfortunately we all make it more difficult for ourselves by being down a lot of the time and by doubting ourselves and blaming others, complaining about our woes, feeling miserable and so on. We are, as you will soon discover, our own worst enemies, as we are using this very same ability against ourselves.

We create our own reality

As I said, we create our own personal realities. It's a bummer eh? As Michael Jackson said, it all starts with the Man in the Mirror. My apologies to the opposite sex, I assure you I am not being sexist. The fact is, the Universe that we exist within, is fundamentally all about creation and we are all part of that creation and we are all individual creators and assist everyday in shaping not only our own lives but also in turn the Universe.

So we have a choice, and life is all about choices, as we can use our free will. As you will see we can choose to be our own worst enemy or our very best friend. Sounds easy eh or maybe a little scary for some but the reality is that the rules are very simple. Applying them and sticking to them is where the real challenge lies, just like in any game.

Even in psychological terms it is recognised that we choose to be exactly where we are at with every decision we make whether we like it or not. And if you don't like it, then once again it's simple, make different choices and you will find yourself in a different place.

If I was sitting in front of you just now I would brace myself as initially, few are ready or willing to accept that they chose every situation in their lives, but when you lead them back through the series of choices they have made, it all becomes shockingly clear. Life doesn't need to be as difficult as we make it; we choose to make it that way.

The Magic of the Universe

I have been screamed at when sharing this point, with *how dare you, how could you possibly think for a second that I chose this or that, you don't know anything about me*. I don't, but I know the rules so I am confident that if given the chance to get to know you I could demonstrate how your choices have shaped you and led you to this point. A famous philosopher once said *my life has been full of pain, trauma and tragedy, 99% of which existed only in my head*. Why?

Fundamentally we in the main, as the body of man, wish to avoid taking responsibility for our actions and this coupled with fear encourages you to take short term pleasure even though you know it will lead to long term pain. You *choose* short-term pleasure.

Some may say they are compelled to out of a need or addiction. This is due to the building of neural pathways in the brain and the emotional chemicals and feelings they release but all, yes all, were started by a thought and in turn a choice fuelled by a desire.

So once again you chose it and you can un-choose it just by making different choices and building new neural pathways by finding something that is so compelling that you are able to block out the emotional dependencies or chemical fixes you got from the old pathways. Just in case you are sitting there thinking *easy for you to say*, let me share more of my truth.

As stated and highlighted at the outset by JJ in the foreword, I have been searching for as long as I can remember for the answer to the burning question on most people's lips, why am I here? What is the purpose of my existence? In my case I was deeply troubled with life and did not seem to fit in, despite appearing to others as attractive, intelligent, gifted and successful.

This led to a preoccupation with suicide, a volatile temperament, and abuse of my gifted intellect and awareness by overreacting to situations and inflicting verbal psychological abuse on others. Thankfully, it was rarely physical, although I accept that psychological scars can be even more difficult to heal.

However, without adding a further negative, the first two weapons in my armoury generally proved to be more than enough and the fear of what may or may not happen next generally stopped the majority of people in their tracks.

This was especially effective because of my look, which was in reality more in my eyes than anything else, although I must admit I did have a menacing appearance in general and coupled with the fact that they didn't quite understand what was going on but felt it deep inside, invariably what they were confronted with verbally was more than enough.

This is called projection and I abused my gift by projecting KEEP AWAY in very loud and menacing terms. The irony was that I wanted the complete opposite, I wanted to be loved and wanted people close to me, so yes, I was very much my own worst enemy and created my own reality, a sad and painful truth which took some time for me to accept, in fact, most of my life.

It's all an illusion

Getting back to the theme, some say that the world and the Universe as we know it or should I say perceive it, is an illusion. Now this could be classed as an unfortunate way to start explaining things as most see the world as a very solid and real place, well I am about to demonstrate that it isn't quite what it seems.

Yes you and I can bang on the wall or the table and hold our loved ones and drive the car and so on, which all seems very real and solid. BUT, and it's a big BUT, there are things that we have now accepted in our everyday lives that actually prove to us that nothing is as solid as we think, so is it an illusion?

When Columbus arrived in the Americas, it is said that the Native American Indians could not see the ships on the horizon, as they had nothing in their world that they could be associated with so they just could not see them, their brains eliminated them from their vision as if they had a built in Photoshop.

The Shaman of the tribe saw ripples and knew that something was causing them so day after day he stared out at the sea trying to work out what was causing them until finally, his brain accepted it.

Given the status and trust of the Shaman, the tribe accepted his word and then they too could see what he saw.

This is a pretty profound point with huge implications for us i.e. we can only see what we believe we can see. Let me expand on this. The brain allegedly processes some 400 billion pieces of information every second, but we are only aware of around 2000, and those 2000 are dealing with the body, our environment, and so on. So are our eyes and nerves seeing and feeling more but we for whatever reason are not permitted to see it?

It would appear to make sense that we can in fact see and sense everything, that we have shared abilities with fellow species on the planet and more, but we have either created or been given filters that only permit that which is deemed necessary to allow us to focus on our purpose so as not to be overwhelmed by billions of pieces of information. Mediums, Clairvoyants and Spiritualists have either learned or had some of those filters removed, hence the reason they see and feel what they do.

What is real?

Most of us know already that we have a robotic aspect to us, the robot that takes over and instructs us to breathe, the heart to pump and so on. It also takes over on long car journeys where you have no recollection of the actual journey but you still drove and arrived safely at your destination. So how much information is the robot being presented with and what are we being sheltered from or excluded from?

Another interesting fact is that the brain does not differentiate between what the eyes see and what it has stored in its memory or created by the imagination. This also has profound implications as it means we have no built in mechanism that separates what we call reality or what we see, from what we imagine. It's like when you return from holiday without photographs, you could quite easily think you just imagined it all. You are trained to think rationally and exclude and differentiate between what appears to be reality and what is not. Has that training been misplaced or is it misleading, intentionally or otherwise?

When I meditate, I don't see things in the conventional sense, I feel the pictures. If I try to see the pictures as if through my eyes they dissipate, but if I leave it, I can see and sense them in my mind.

There was a documentary recently, which highlighted the case of a man who was blind in one eye. The researchers covered his good eye and subjected him to a series of lines on a screen and asked him to state the direction the lines were going in, up, down, right or left. He was able to tell them and get it right every single time, 100% of the time no less. When they asked how he could do it, he felt he *was* guessing but the indications were from the scans used that he *could* somehow *see* using what we might refer to as the third eye.

When scientists delve into the brain, they can find no evidence of the observer, the "I", the self that uses the brain and looks through the eyes. It's no wonder as the "I" is an energy being, so we have an intangible being observing our world and it cannot discern what has been imagined or what has been seen. So what is real and what is reality?

We have very good examples of this that are easier to grasp. When first presented with 3D pictures all you see is a collage of colours, however when told what to do and explained that there is an image within, you can suddenly and spontaneously see a 3D image appear right before your eyes. Now that image was always there, you just needed to be told and to believe it was there before you could actually see it.

Likewise with the inverted mask, when you look at it your brain shows you a face, it is only when you go to touch the face you discover that the face is not protruding as you at first believed, but is in fact inverted.

I think I have made my point and stimulated your thinking and I will leave it at that for the moment as I have no intention of taking you down the worm hole any deeper as I promised to keep this simple and I acknowledge that some of the numbers we have used and are about to use are in themselves incomprehensible and so large that they become absolutely meaningless i.e. 400 billion per second,

50 billion planets and so on. What it does do is paint a picture and creates an element of scale and scale and perspective is very important.

Seeking the truth

We must also learn from history. Man has always made assumptions and created myths believed them to be true and shared this *en masse*, like the earth is flat, which few actually believed, as have been many other shared assumptions.

Interestingly the ancients knew the answers, including the fact that the world was not flat, but were ignored or worse, discriminated against and their wisdom hidden from the masses. Why? In whose interests was it to create control by ignoring the old beliefs?

Fortunately science is once again proving the old ways to be true and science and spiritualism do appear to be merging, which begs the question, where are those in denial of the true magic of the Universe going to seek sanctuary now?

A Tibetan monk when asked what he thought, having been exposed to western civilisation, said he was surprised by how much they had regressed. Note he said regressed and not progressed. So is life an illusion? Are we all in a great star trek holodeck or are we individual programmers in the matrix? To a certain extent, yes, we are all creators, so read on and let's look at how it all works.

Let's bring things back into our day to day reality for a moment. How does your mobile phone work indoors? How do X-rays and cat scans show things we cannot see? The reason being, and we have to accept this, is that nothing is solid. Some things are just denser than other things but nothing is solid.

I know it's hard to grasp. Let me try and make it easier and clearer to picture and imagine and at the same time start to show you the how and why of the Universe.

The Magic of the Universe

Everything in this whole Universe is made up of what some scientists might call quanta, the basis behind quantum physics which is turning the old science on its head. Now I am no scientist so forgive me if I miss something, but basically, in quantum mechanics, one cannot predict what something will do in the future, only the probability.

Not only that, how about the notion that this energy flashes in and out of existence and relies on a conscious observer in order for it to appear to exist at all.

This stuff is what permeates and penetrates the whole of the Universe and is the basis from which all things are made. Protons, electrons, neutrons and atoms, all descriptive words to describe minute energies that are attracted to each other and held together by vibration to form things. If these were to be drawn to a scale so that you could see them then you would see that they were the equivalent of about a football pitch apart. Even the nucleus is not solid.

So, we have established that nothing is solid, in fact the Universe is pretty empty and the impression of solid material things are an illusion of sorts, it's just energy vibrating at different frequencies in and out of view depending on who is watching. The lower the vibration, the denser the thing, the higher the vibration, the lighter and more transparent the thing, until it cannot be seen by the naked eye, or can it?

Now the fascinating thing about quanta, other than it fills the whole Universe, is that it behaves as a wave until observed and then it behaves as a particle, so it has the ability to react, which is as I say, fascinating.

One must also ask the question, when this particle flashes in and out of view, where does it go? Well the belief is that it can exist in more than one place at the same time. They also reckon the best way to describe this energy is possibility, or thought, and that thought or possibility can exist in many dimensions until it is shaped and it then collapses in on one.

Wild as this may seem they have actually been able to recreate this in labs. When people have been shown this type of demonstration in experiments they are under whelmed, they fail to grasp that it is the same object in two places at the same time. I suppose it would be more impressive if they could do it with a human, which is obviously a possibility as everything is in fact possible, this would no doubt create a more animated reaction, but the true magnitude of the implications take time to be grasped as most would assume that it was a clone or a duplicate and not the same thing. We truly struggle to comprehend this.

So this energy that permeates and makes up the Universe reacts to being observed. Now most of us will also truly struggle to grasp this but sometimes as I have said before, you just know or feel the truth. What is compelling is that the great thinkers and philosophers throughout history have often made fantastic assumptions, or did they know or have access to something we have lost or misplaced about the nature of the Universe, just as the Greek or Egyptian philosophers did thousands of years ago? Science now appears to be reaching the same conclusions and as a result spreading the understanding to additional people who will find it more palatable given that they see it as coming from a more "reliable" source.

Science versus Magic

At this juncture I will digress slightly to highlight a point about what has gone before versus what we are discovering now i.e. science versus magic or ancient wisdom, and why it all points to the fact that the answers have always been out there. Well, in the terms that we understand always.

For example, as part of the ongoing analysis of the long term effects of astronauts spending extended periods in Space, NASA discovered that the skin appeared to have different energy points. They mapped this with their super computers and discovered what the ancients had known for thousands of years, acupuncture points, the energy grid of the body. Think about that for a moment, science with its super computers is proving what has been known for thousands of years.

Likewise with true astrology, which is gaining greater and greater acceptance as a useful science today, including in the commercial world such as merchant banking where it is used to monitor trends. I am not referring to the fixed sun signs that most papers and magazines carry, but chart driven astrology. However it is interesting to note that the world still carries such things as fixed sun signs in its publications.

I was first introduced to true astrology some 14 years ago when I had my own chart done. I was so blown away with the results that I used a management consultancy firm that I owned at the time to carry out an experiment, basically to compare astrology with psychometric analysis. I asked the astrologer to complete a form in a similar style to the psychometric analysis as I did not wish to know any personal details.

Six clients agreed to take part providing nothing more than date, and place and time of birth for the astrology, and they all undertook the standard psychometric tests. The accuracy of the astrology blew the psychometric tests away. The point is, as I said earlier, that the answers are already out there.

One question to keep in mind for the moment is who told people about acupuncture and astrology given the monumental task involved in creating such things from scratch, even with today's super computers, yet the ancients knew all about it? Just like the Egyptians and Sirius B. Who told them? How did it start? Why did it start? Why did we forget?

The ancients and ancient wisdom

It is worth spending a few moments more on this as it is very relevant and helps makes some sense of everything. In our current existence we talk about the ancients as those people who existed in Egyptian / Mayan or Greek history and see people before this time as being distinctly primitive. However we somewhat arrogantly ignore the fact that those recent day ancients i.e. Egyptians etc all talk of older civilisations that were far superior to them, who they learned from.

In fact some say that man in his various forms has been around for millennia and civilisations have come and gone. Now we may say where is the evidence for this? Well we have touched upon this above with astrology, acupuncture, calendars, sharing of knowledge etc. etc. none of which ties in with what we believed was possible within the so called primitive world.

A couple of things to ponder upon, in my opinion a true advance in civilisation and technology would be that which lives in harmony with the environment its home, its mother earth etc. Yes some of our advances seem miraculous; however most are fatally flawed as they are either unsustainable or downright damaging to the environment.

This links in with my next point and that is that if the previous civilisations were further advanced then it could be that their technology was more in tune with the environment so when their civilisation ceased for whatever reason and more on that much later, their technology was re absorbed. There is also the distinct possibility that evidence does exist and is buried or hidden as one would expect by the ever shifting oceans and geology. Our investigations of the ocean beds and below the ice caps are minimal to say the least and all were once inhabited, who knows what secrets they would expose.

If our civilisation was to experience a cataclysmic event what would survive what would be sustainable, would we revert to a so called primitive life in tune with the environment or endeavour to resurrect things or a combination of both. Considering all this helps us see that it is very possible that civilisations could have existed before and been wiped out and started again, why, well more on that later, I just wanted to get my definition of ancients into perspective, I am referring to the same ancients that the Egyptians etc. referred to.

We are all energy

Getting back to our quanta, some people have labelled it the thinking stuff as if it can react it must be able to think on some level and scientists have confirmed that it can exist in multi dimensions. So we have energy, a vibration, a thinking stuff, that permeates the whole Universe and all things are made of this. This forms the basis of all that I am going to share with you throughout this book as this combined with our desire and imagination shapes everything in our existence.

So you should be starting to get a flavour, a taste of how we are all magicians, all creators. I have purposely avoided religious or biblical terms so far, but will as a matter of course have to deal with it, but for the moment let's look at this once again as it is so critical. I will summarise everything in a few lines.

We have energy, a vibration, a thinking stuff, that permeates the whole Universe and all things are made of this. This is the basis of all that I am going to share with you throughout this book and combined with our desire and imagination it is what shapes everything in our existence.

This reaffirms what I stated earlier that what separates us is Desire and Imagination and we create not only our own reality but the Universe as a result, and that the Universe is designed to encourage this as its main purpose is creation.

The quanta does not just act as a particle when observed it reacts to our thoughts or should I more accurately say it is shaped by our thoughts, especially when our thoughts are at the correct frequency or vibration.

So with our desire and imagination can we influence the quantum that in turn brings what we desire into existence? YES, however and there has to be a however, there are safeguards or

The Magic of the Universe

obstacles and rules, just like in any game, all of which make good sense when you are presented with them.

You may now start to get a glimpse of why life is the Ultimate Game and despite the enormous numbers, quantum physics and philosophies involved, fortunately when you strip it all back it's all very simple, we have chosen to make it complicated to justify our existence and trying to compete is one of the traps of the game.

So let's consider this further for a moment. Everything is made of quanta or energy, a vibration, thinking stuff, rocks, plants – everything. If this is what makes everything, then this means everything is also capable of thought, and in turn memory at some level as quanta is thinking stuff or thought energy, and in turn everything is connected, and therefore all that separates conscious communication with everything else is the different levels of vibration.

There has been a recent scientific breakthrough that highlights the communication via vibration and frequency that is related to powering objects with wireless electricity. This is achieved by sharing resonant frequencies. So what else could be possible by obtaining the correct vibration or frequency? Most people will struggle with the fact that electricity can travel safely without wires and without being seen, far less anything else.

However, what we in fact are discovering is that everything in the Universe is speaking the same language but depending on its level of vibration it speaks so slowly or softly or with such basic vocabularies that unless you vibrate at a level close to it you won't consciously understand it. I say consciously as at another level you will feel it. This is how psychics and mediums work. There are many demonstrable cases where a medium has picked up an inanimate object, including rocks, and been able to tell its history. They have the ability to tune into that frequency and vibration.

The ancients knew this and so do those that still follow the old ways, certain tribes for example, still practice this. They can communicate with plants, trees, animals and so on to know where food is and what is edible. This makes a lot of sense to me.

I have always been baffled by the thought that who on earth first decided after suddenly stumbling across an octopus or a squid or some other equally attractive species that they would eat it? Not only would they eat it, but how did they know it was safe to eat? Likewise with all bugs and roots, there has to have been either an original teacher or some form of communication. Everything therefore has a memory.

Thoughts are energy

As I have said I'm not a scientist, I am merely sharing what I understand after listening to scientists giving interviews. In our own case the cells that make up our bodies, of which there are approximately 100 Trillion of them, all contain sufficient information to recreate our whole bodies and despite the minute size of these cells, they in turn have thousands of receptors on them.

Again doing the maths, the numbers get huge. We can therefore be likened to our own Universes just by considering the huge numbers and complexities that make up a single human being. Peptides which carry the chemicals that give us emotions are released by thoughts so we are in fact a carbon machine that produces proteins and the chemicals to reproduce all emotions.

These peptides generated by thoughts land on the cells and like homeopathic medicine, imprint on the cells. Now this is replicated each time the cell splits, once again this has profound implications for our bodies as it means that thoughts shape our bodies as they impact the cells.

Even more interesting is that as the cells that have been impacted split and replicate, they take this with them, increasing the emotional aspect or need, and at the same time becoming less effective as a cell and this is what results in ageing. So whilst we can and do affect our bodies by what we eat and how we act, the biggest impact is created by what we think.

This is a very important area to focus on for a moment as thought not only produces peptides it also creates neural pathways.

The more we think the greater the pathway becomes, this becomes self fulfilling, as the more we think the more peptides are released to encourage us as it gives as an emotional fix and the easier it becomes because of the increased neural pathways and so it becomes addictive.

We can therefore become addicted to being our own worst enemy or best friend, it is that simple but equally that difficult as anyone that has tried to give up an addiction will know. But the key is that it is all thought driven, we chose it and we can choose to change it just by changing our thoughts and now that you know this you can start immediately.

Now as thoughts are not created by the brain but by the "I", the self, the observer, the energy body, the spirit that inhabits the body, then it's the spirit that requires to be dealt with to control the thoughts. We are now getting closer to why we are here and what the game is all about.

A word about God

It is at this juncture given the discussions surrounding spirit that I must bring in God to help explain things further. I will avoid a detailed explanation at this point as it can be covered in other more appropriate sections. However it would seem unrealistic to be talking about the Universe and what makes it work without some mention of God as this is a universal reference point for all whether you are religious or not.

I have to say that I do not possess the intellect or literary skills to adequately describe this so for the moment I will keep it simple and once again make reference to ancient teachings that help make sense of things. I also do not feel qualified to speak about God in any depth so with that in mind, I would prefer to refer to God as Good, as I'm sure we can all agree that whatever your beliefs, God is associated with doing good. God or Good, in whatever form you wish to relate, created everything and everything as a result is part of God, therefore the all conscious, all connected Universe is Good.

The Magic of the Universe

Good created man in his or her image, there is no sexual differentiation in the Universe, all things have male energy and all things have female energy, everything has yin and yang. By creating man in his own likeness means we have the ability to create like Good. Good is within us all and the ability to create is within every single one of us.

Good made this possible by separating us and by arming us with the tools of desire and imagination. The ultimate desire is to return to Good, the source of all things. This leads us temporarily onto other aspects before I move onto what the rules are and what the protections are.

So what is mankind? Are we physically in the form of Good? No! Our bodies are a shell, a protective casing that we utilise when we are on the earthly plane or earthly dimension. Quite literally our bodies are our temples and very sophisticated temples as well, that act as the ultimate transmitters and receivers.

We are all spiritual beings that inhabit this earth for an allotted time to serve a purpose, that purpose is ultimately to learn and grow, to create and experience, all of which is retained and stored in the all consciousness.

There is an evolutionary cycle that is followed, it began with a universal spiritual consciousness and this evolved to a species specific consciousness and then self consciousness and so on and the circle is closed as we evolve back to the universal consciousness and so it goes on and on as we evolve for the benefit of all things.

It is my belief that we come to earth through choice as a spirit who wishes to learn and grow or get closer to Good and to do so we must shed all negativity. You will now see the link between the spirit, thoughts, and the impact on the body and in turn the Universe around it.

The purer the thought, the more positive is the impact on the body and the Universe. Most dis-eases are best cured at the source, through the spirit, the thought, rather than to treat the manifestation in the body, hence the reason remote healing works, as does the placebo effect.

We actually choose what lessons we wish to learn and who we will learn them from and even the circumstances that are created to allow that to happen. BUT, to ensure the lessons are well learned and deeply rooted we are given a handicap, a very serious handicap, called Free Will.

Free will gives us the ability to choose what we do on the earthly plane. We are further handicapped in that most cannot remember why they came or what lessons or tasks they set themselves as that would spoil the game, and for the lesson to be truly learned one needs to choose to learn it and experience the implications of cause and effect. You could in fact, keep repeating the mistakes so back you keep coming. It would also appear to be critical that we experience, hence the reason that we need this carbon body that produces chemical emotional reactions, so that we can FEEL the outcome.

So why do we need to come to earth, or a planet? We do so as it's the safest way to experiment, experience and learn. Let's eliminate one HUGE question here and now about Good and the Universe which will help make sense of it all, and we can expand on it later.

We are all made in the image of Good which means we are all energy beings that are immortal and we exist for infinity, getting closer and closer to the source until we are as one. Therefore we cannot and do not die. Death is an illusion. What in fact happens is we transfer from one level to another and hopefully keep climbing the ladder of levels until we reach the source of ultimate Good.

I used to struggle with aspects of a God, Godhead, Universal Being, superior being etc. etc. Until I started to reflect on what I did accept and expanded upon that. We have discussed how our bodies are made up of trillions of cells and receptors all passing information to a central source and that the brain apparently processes billions of pieces of information in a second, not just from a body functioning aspect but also from a sensory perceptive taking in everything in our environment and further compounded by the thought process and recognition. So on that level we accept that in order to function we deal with billions of pieces of information in a second.

The Magic of the Universe

Is it that much of a leap to take that further and say that 6.5 billion people a much smaller figure are all connected in a central consciousness, especially one that is far more evolved than we can even imagine. We readily accept that things are made of atoms, electrons and protons and now quanta but we cannot see them, we accept the evidence presented and accept that physics still cannot explain our world. So why can we not accept that there is more than we can see, that we are all part of a functioning universe and all connected.

Why are we here?

Given that we cannot die then we must ask why we are here at all on this level. The reason being is that the safeguards that exist on this plane make it safe for us to play the game and not mess up the Universe with our badly controlled desires and imagination. So if you want, it's like a giant soft play centre for mankind, a virtual reality game where you think someone has gone but in fact like the virtual reality game they can reappear, in our reality it would be in the form of reincarnation in another lifetime.

The ancients stated that man arrived in purely spirit form initially and as they evolved into the earthly plane and took form in a material sense they became denser and at a lower vibration. At the risk of pushing the boundaries further we apparently were giants initially in comparison to the form we have now and that would seem to tie in with the size of the species in millennia passed. We also retained what we refer to as the third eye, however this proved a distraction as seeing the astral or other worlds became less important in the game of experience. With each evolutionary cycle we became smaller and denser and had less use of the third eye.

On the astral plane whatever you desire or imagine appears in an instant, so imagine the chaos if there was no order or control to this? Fortunately there is order and control and I will expand on this in other chapters but in the meantime please stay with me and read on. So on the earthly plane we retain the ability to create what we want but there is another safety valve built in called TIME.

The Magic of the Universe

Time was created in this dimension only. It does not exist in any other dimension and it exists purely in this dimension to put a distance between the initial desire, thought and imagination and the action, to ensure that you are consistent in your desire, intent and actions.

Take a moment to contemplate that and see how much sense it makes. If everything happened in an instant imagine the chaos. On how many occasions have you been pleased that you had the time to rethink before you did something? Equally, it's a discipline to ensure that what you desire remains consistent.

Merely desiring something is not sufficient, it must also be consistent and you must raise your thought vibration to the level of the thinking stuff, the quanta, in order that your communication is understood and whatever you imagine or shape can in turn be shaped by the Universe.

Whilst there are exercises and steps and procedures that can be followed to assist with this such as meditation and visualisation, the fact is that the vibration that you emit when grateful and happy is in tune with the quanta so if you can stay in that state of mind then you can communicate and create your hearts desire.

You will recall that I stated at the outset that the irony was that the happier and more lighthearted you are, the easier it is to create your desires. Now you know why. It is because the vibration emitted at that level is in tune with the Universe.

The Universe delivers exactly what you ask for

At this point I am reminded of the story of the temple of the 1,000 mirrors.

A dog wanders aimlessly into a temple that contains 1,000 mirrors and is immediately confronted with 1,000 dogs looking back at him. His hackles go up and so do theirs, he snarls and they snarl back and so it goes on until the dog drives itself into such frenzy that it drops dead of a heart attack.

The Magic of the Universe

A few days later another dog wanders in and is confronted by the very same thing, but this dog wags its tail, and the more he does the more they wag theirs, and eventually a very happy and contented dog leaves the temple.

The Universe is like the temple, it does not question, it merely reflects and delivers what you say or act that you want. It is not evil, it doesn't judge, it delivers what you consistently say you want, it does not make decisions for you and it does not scale. It does, however, have another controlling mechanism that we can call Karma, whereby your deeds are reflected back to you, sometimes instantly, sometimes over lifetimes, but every deed, action or thought, creates cause and effect or action and reaction.

I can hear you say *what about all the guys that stole and killed etc to get what they wanted and they got away with it?* Well we will deal with that and much more sensitive subjects too, but for now it is enough to know that nobody escapes Karma.

There is also far too much emphasis on money and accumulating money and when you grasp all that I am saying you will see how misplaced and man made an illusion this is.

I also mentioned earlier that our bodies are like great transmitters and receivers, our skeleton acts like an aerial and our bodies are made up of 90% water, as you probably know, a great conductor.

Water is one of the most receptive elements in the Universe. Scientific tests have shown that pure distilled water can be affected by merely attaching a word or label to the water container (thought, spoken or written) and the water is changed at a molecular level also when blessed so imagine what our thoughts do to us and those around us.

For some reason the children's saying of *sticks and stones can break my bones but words can never hurt me* comes to mind. It would appear that this has either been misquoted, just as the saying that money is the root of all evil, actually is the love of money is the root of all evil, and if it is not misquoted then it's clearly wrong.

Why? Well let's follow the logic if thoughts are things and if water, of which we are mostly made up, can be changed with a label or a thought, then both the name calling or labelling and the thought behind it does have an impact, an effect, so can potentially hurt if the person allows it to, with the extreme version of such words known as a curse, so once again a lesson in harbouring pure thoughts and sharing positive words.

Can we now see how truly interconnected we are as we are passing and receiving billions of pieces of information per second.

The Universe impacts on us hence the reason astrology works, why moods are affected by the full moon, and we in turn affect the Universe and those around us. The magic or the universe is working all the time 24/7 whether we want it to or not.

Dreaming and out of body experience

I must also spend some time on the importance of dreams in both the psychological aspect and the spiritual aspect. We have stated that the brain does not differentiate between what it sees, what it remembers, and what it imagines, and it is bombarded with 400 billion bits of info every second, but we are only consciously aware of 2000 or so.

What happens to the colossal amount of information that we are not aware of is obviously the subject of some speculation as if it is not in the conscious mind then it would be fair to assume it must be in the subconscious.

In psychological terms our dreams are used to deal with the information stored in the subconscious and this information is played back to us and sorted through dreams. Dreams therefore play a crucial role in our mental health, dealing with issues that we have avoided consciously.

It is also recognised and accepted that you can dream solutions in a controlled fashion by requesting this before you sleep, and this has been a feature of my life. I have regularly been presented with insights and how to do things within my dreams. Some have been very practical and I could easily relate to them. Others have been more science fiction like and downright bizarre ranging from being shown perpetual motion propulsion using magnetic fields to antimatter.

In fact, if you look into the genesis of many groundbreaking ideas, the innovators often state that they dreamt the solution or it came to them when they were not consciously thinking about it. Tesla and Einstein are two excellent examples.

In spiritual terms, dreams are when we connect with the astral planes and one of the reasons our bodies are immobilised, other than it would be dangerous if our bodies acted out our dreams, is so that our astral body is free to explore the astral planes. The driver has left the vehicle behind if you like, and therefore what we think we have dreamt is in fact our experiences during those explorations. Our brains try to make sense of these adventures in the only way it knows how, by putting together a series of images, possibilities and events gleaned from experience.

This explains for me many of my dreams, where I have felt some one I knew was in my dream, but I did not recognise them physically, I can only presume what I was sensing was that person's astral body in another reincarnation or dimension.

I personally had a validated out of body experience in my teenage years. I was suddenly aware that I was standing on the corner of my street and I could see my friend Gary standing at the corner kissing a girl. This was a shock as Gary had never had a girlfriend and the girl he was kissing was slightly older than him, which was a big thing in the teenage years. I called out to Gary a few times and had a sudden realisation that he could neither hear nor see me. At the same moment I remembered that I was at home sleeping and I felt a rush of wind and what I can only describe as an intense flickering and buzzing and woke with my mother coming into my room asking if I was ok.

Later on in the week I was sitting in the local pub with the boys when one said that he thought that Gary had "pulled" at the weekend which as I say was news, as up to that point he had not had a girlfriend. I blurted out *yes I know* and named the girl just as Gary arrived. He reluctantly confirmed this and later told me that he had been standing on that corner at that time. I am pleased to say that as far as I'm aware, they are still together nearly 30 years later.

Some friends have claimed that I visit them at night. I have no memory or dream that coincides with these statements but I trust them sufficiently to accept their comments and beliefs as I too have been convinced that certain people have joined me or been present and admittedly I only sensed and felt their presence, I didn't see them in the conventional sense.

My son Scott has experienced similar things and was awakened one night because of the banging of the window in his bedroom. As he awoke, he saw Shona, my ex wife and his step mum, holding it shut and telling him to go back to sleep. When he got up in the morning he remembered that Shona was away on business and was shocked at what he firmly believed he saw and heard.

Those practiced in astral projection and out of body experiences have demonstrated in experiments that they have been able to visit remote locations and not only report back accurately what they saw but also hold conversations with the people there.

Interestingly those people were in the main not consciously aware of holding the conversations with the astral wanderer, so it would appear that the communications were held astral to astral. Both the USA and Russian military are believed to use astral projection and out of body practitioners within their military arsenal, they are known as "remote viewers".

It is easier for me to grasp and accept these concepts as I have had direct experience of them, whether in vivid dreams or projection, the key for me here is the word experience. This seems to be a very important aspect. It would seem that we have the ability to exist within a mental thought world but actual experience is important, even though we do not appear to be able to differentiate it within our brains.

Dreaming has been a very useful and powerful tool in my tool box although I have to say that my dreams have influenced my moods during waking hours, not always in a positive fashion, particularly if I had a negative or confusing dream about a person or situation.

There are a number of books on the subject of dreams and this should come as no surprise. In fact I am surprised that there are not more given the amount of time we spend in the dream state and the important role it plays, whether you believe in the spiritual aspect or not.

I am personally not in favour of dream books that make over simplistic statements such as if you dream of a dog it has a particular meaning. I accept that there may be an ancient wisdom that can accurately relate the symbolism but I think that this is being misrepresented, just as astrology is with the presentation of the sun sign messages making it look like all Arians will experience the same thing on the same day etc, which sadly belittles the signs and skills of the true astrologers who can chart ones possibilities. I therefore favour what I will label the alien approach.

Imagine you were describing your dream to an alien that had never experienced earth or our ways or cultures and everything had to be explained. You would have to then look at what the symbols meant to you. You may love dogs, you may be scared of dogs, you may have killed a dog, been rescued by a dog, and so on about anything. Look at the related significance and then try and explain it to someone who had never seen or experienced such things, try explaining it to an alien.

I also believe that we can transcend time in dreams, hence déjà vu, and recognition of places that you have never visited in the conscious world. This should be an obvious aspect to leaving the time bound physical plane and accessing the astral plane which is not time bound. Science knows that it is theoretically possible to go back in time and to bend time but it is the implications of this on the earthly plane that stumps them.

So dreams and sleep play a huge part in our lives, it is obviously much more than just recuperation, we are still gathering, receiving, and projecting information, and travelling to different planes and dimensions.

Gut feelings

The multi layer multi dimension and interconnected aspects of the Universe can also be demonstrated by a simple pendulum diviner, which can be used like divining rods to trace things, and different lengths can be used to identify different materials or elements.

That in itself is fascinating and something we can all easily try, however not only can it also be used remotely to identify and position by using the pendulum over a map, but as you go above a certain length the pendulum still works for the different materials and elements, only now it reacts slightly offset indicating different dimensions, which once again ties in all the theories in quantum physics and ancient philosophies.

All that I am saying will either feel right to you or not and I have stated that we all intuitively and instinctively feel the truth, our gut feeling, and what I have said will either make sense to you or feel worthy of further exploration or it wont.

Keeping with the gut feeling for a moment, it is interesting that our feeling does not emanate from the brain. When you say something feels right or you sense it, it does not feel right in the brain, but in your gut, your core. The reason for this is that this temple of a body that we inhabit, this great receiver and transmitter, plays a role that few understand, but once again the ancients did, hence the reason that they were able to create acupuncture thousands of years ago, knew about reflexology, and so and on.

They also said that the liver was a very important organ as it housed the soul and reflected one world to another. Interestingly, if you were to witness an operation you would see that the liver is in fact reflective and looks like a mirror. So is this why we feel what we feel in the gut, or should I say the liver?

Healing and Modern Medicine

Keeping with the theme of the ancients and our bodies and the fact that our thoughts create our internal and external realities, it would appear that our reliance today on modern medicines is more to do with money than to do with healing. What I mean by this is that you cannot patent something that is naturally occurring, therefore you cannot make vast sums of money from it, so naturally occurring remedies are not promoted and through time, the vast majority of us might forget that they even exist so won't even know we can try them.

I am reminded of a slightly obscure example re passing of time and forgetting things, but it's what has popped into my head so there must be a reason for it. Santa Claus is generally accepted as wearing red clothes, where in fact this was part of a marketing ploy by Coca Cola which is now accepted as the norm. There are many other day to day examples of things that we accept without remembering the original intent or message. Santa Claus may appear a flippant example but it just goes to show what can happen.

I am not against modern day medicine, I just recognise the fact that what we are presented with is not necessarily always the best solution, but often the most profitable or most marketed. There is, however, an increasingly growing trend to what is labelled alternative medicine, or new age medicine, which is ironic given its ancient roots, as modern medicine struggles to find the solutions.

The answers generally already exist in nature, but in our arrogance we have tried to improve on nature, compete with it, make money out of it, rather than learn from it, and this has been as a result of chasing the illusion of material gain.

Once again the evidence of nature playing its role is all around us if we care to open our eyes to it. I remember someone excitedly telling me that you can cure hay fever by eating locally produced honey. This may at first seem amazing but is in fact very logical given it's the same pollen that creates the hay fever so it's all part of a cycle.

The Magic of the Universe

What surprises me more is why we don't automatically expand this thinking and recognise not only the naturally occurring remedies but the fact that the remedies would not be required at all if we lived in harmony with our surroundings. The drive for goods and stuff and profit means that our supermarkets are full of produce from all over the world and with very little of it home grown, and in the majority of cases chemically enhanced to increase shelf life. No wonder our immune systems and natural antibodies and defences are confused.

I went to sleep one night contemplating this subject and the message I got was interesting and is worth sharing. It was that the body struggles with food stuffs that have been adapted by man, like saturated and hydrogenated fats for example. It's like putting the wrong fuel in a car as it just isn't cut out for the job and eventually will clog up the engine.

We are no different. In fact our engines are even more sophisticated and sensitive than other vehicles. We may carry out tests to ensure something is safe on one level but we fail to see the bigger picture and the long term implications, although at least now, the so called experts are recognising that saturated fat should be eliminated from our diets.

This reminds me of an old acquaintance who said that science can look at a spot on the knee of a fly but in turn forgets it's a fly that it is looking at. I.e. by forgetting that there is a bigger picture we end up taking a pill to counter act a pill and never deal with the actual problem.

I can share a practical example. I was working on a tunnel repair and required a temporary support system so that we could safely repair a certain section. The design team set to work and a few weeks later the steel work arrived on site. It was impressive but very heavy. I called the design team and asked how I was meant to erect it. They quoted a certain crane as ideal. I reminded them that I was in a tunnel. There was silence at the other end and we had to get the burning gear out so that we could get small enough sections. The design was great but they had not looked at the bigger picture and all its implications. This applies in life when we get so close that we can't see what's around us.

Interestingly for me is that when I started to fully embrace all that I write in the book, and the writing of the book itself, my health has never been better and I feel the youngest I have ever felt. It is also worth touching on age for a moment.

Age is another illusion. We never feel any older, the "I", the self, the observer, is ageless, it is our bodies that age, ironically it would appear, as a result of our thoughts. We all know at a deep level that we are ageless, timeless, and immortal, in fact if our bodies did not age the importance of experience would be elevated to its true position into our consciousness.

Open your mind and unlock the doors to possibility

So as I draw to the conclusion of this chapter, I hope that I have opened your eyes to the size, magnitude, variety, and magic of the Universe, and how we are all interconnected and can influence it as it does us.

I hope I have demonstrated that we are different from most species by way of desire and imagination, and given you a taster of how we actually shape our own realities by the uncontrolled use of this desire and imagination, and that time was created to help us play the game, and finally, karma ensures that we can never escape the consequences of our desires, imagination and actions.

In order to play the game and get the maximum from it you need the discipline to practice as you would any game, and like any top athlete you should always be open to accept the guidance of experienced coaches in the game.

I will list all the exercise and steps you can do to become proficient and if you think you have learned enough to start then you can skip right to them and start working your way through them. However, I have kept this book purposely short, and I would recommend that you read it all first, as each or any chapter just might contain that missing piece in the jigsaw you require.

For those exploring this topic for the first time I am sure you are brimming with questions and arguments, all of which I will deal with, and if not, there are many detailed books on any of the subjects covered, just ask for them and you will be either drawn to them or them to you.

I think we all intuitively know most of what I am saying, I did, and I know that it's very difficult to explain. You know it's there but when trying to put it all into words it just seems to float out of reach, like trying to grab a cloud perhaps, because we are reaching behind the veil, the filters. I will end this chapter with a few key points.

Key Points

The Universe is creative not competitive so any idea generated that is creative is in tune with the Universe and more likely to succeed.

Whilst I acknowledge that everything is generated from thought I see a significant difference between mechanical, robotic, regurgitated process-led thought playing stuck records, and free thought, open and in tune, non judgemental, imaginative, intuitive thought, as experienced by all the notable greats who may have claimed like I used to, that it was more by accident than by design.

There is no such thing as an accident, everything happens for a reason.

We can all tap into this knowledge and we talk about it in our daily lives without really considering what we are actually referring to when we talk about it. Common sense, something that is common to us and shared by us all, the universal consciousness, and the more that people wake up and tune in, the more others are likely to follow, just like the 100 monkey effect. This phenomenon states that once a critical number is reached, ideas and beliefs can transfer to other members of the population. It originates from observations of the Macaques monkeys where some of the monkeys had learned to wash potatoes and this behaviour spread to other monkeys on other islands once the critical number had been reached.

Competition is a man made thing on this level or dimension, so if you desire something just to beat or outdo someone then you are being negative and competitive. However, if you wish to create something better and more useful to everyone then that is being creative.

Whilst learning to discipline your desires and imagination you are constantly going to be tempted and it is the act of this resistance that generates light in recognition of the positive steps. Physics demonstrates this artificially with light bulbs, the light is

The Magic of the Universe

generated from the resistance and the Universe is no different. In fact the Universe is made of light and you can light up your world by resisting the negative and focusing on the positive.

The Universe and our lives appears to be a large numbers game, it sometimes seems to be the only way we can make sense of things, but at the same time the numbers are so large that they can also seem nonsensical. There are 6.5 billion living souls on this planet. Do you ever truly contemplate this? How that 6.5 billion is made up, what nationalities, what religions, where you fit in, where your religion fits in, where your country fits in?

Do the exercise, it's healthy to scale things to get things back into perspective as all too often your reality is limited to who you can see in the room just now. It's hard to picture the street or the town or city, far less the 6.5 billion that share this planet with you all, all desiring, all imagining, all creating to expand this to the Universe and all things in it.

There are no rights and wrongs, there are only rules and guidelines and endless possibilities, and whilst thought is the source, the power is in the doing.

Act out the creation, live and play the game. I am going to help you, let's start your preparation for the game.

Let there be light.

The Magic of the Universe

Games are about having fun, lightening ones spirit, increasing ones vibration, whilst all the time learning.

Learn to go with the flow

Going with the flow

"In a storm which tree is likely to be uprooted? Is it the one that stands rigid and fights it, or the one that bends in the wind?

Having set the scene in the magic of the Universe, we now see that we can either be our own best friend or worst enemy, given the fact that we all shape and create our own realities. Let us now look at how simple it is to sabotage our desires, or in turn, positively create the life we want and need, in other words, how to play the game successfully.

It's all too easy to look outwards and readily find justification or confusion, and whilst it is much more difficult to take responsibility and look inward, you will reap the benefits. Inner reflection allows you to make more intuitive choices and will reduce noisy distractions leaving you free to focus on you.

I am reminded of a super salesman I recruited as he was deemed to be the best. He told me he was not a salesman but an assistant buyer and he showed me the effect of distraction. He asked what I enjoyed and I said *cars*. He said *if I sat 50 cars in front of you, I bet that rather than being able to focus on the one you favoured the most, all you would end up having is a sore head trying to choose.* He carried on. *However, if I limited the number of cars to just 5, I guarantee a choice and a sale.*

Life is no different, start with you and everything else will follow.

There are a number of phrases that you hear people use regularly, and just like the way many people watch TV, they use them in a robotic, flippant, manner, with little regard to what they are saying, what it actually means, or why they are saying it. For example, I often hear people emit the words; *I will just go with the flow*. Going with the flow is in fact a very powerful statement, as I will elaborate upon, and is often referred to in ancient philosophies and martial arts.

Unfortunately in modern times it tends to be misused as a cop out, a lazy get out clause, once again an attempt to avoid responsibility. For example when asking someone what they are going to do, you might often hear the answer *Ach I will just go with the flow*. Basically it is all too often used to say that you don't know what you want, and worse still, that you don't actually care, and typically, it is said in a very lethargic and laid back manner.

We have discussed that it's the vibration or energy that influences, attracts and shapes or repels energy of a similar vibration, and that thoughts are energy. What we must also consider is the strength of that thought, the depth and consistency, basically the emotion or feeling behind it, the intensity of the intent. Feelings or emotions are very important.

Every message is heard – make it clear

I intimated at the outset of this book that we all intuitively feel or know the truth. We have feelings or emotions about absolutely everything that we say, think, or do, and we must learn to be aware of these feelings, and in turn, trust them, as they are the volume control to the Universe. They also impact on us at a cellular level and it is the lack of control of these feelings, our addiction to certain emotions, which causes accelerated ageing.

So if we have a clear, precise, simple message that we feel good and strong about, it will not only be heard loud and clear, it will have a positive effect on our health and wellbeing also. Every message is heard, but most are either faint or confused and cluttered, so what we get back from the Universe is faint, confused and cluttered, it's that simple.

Verbalising those thoughts is even more powerful as an action has taken place which involved more thoughts and energy to instruct the muscles, so the energy has increased and therefore so has the message to the Universe, and it will either be magnified or neutralised by how you actually feel. Think about that, consider it. Are you magnifying making things easier or are you neutralising and frustrating your life and wasting energy?

Let's look at how a message, an action and the associated feelings can be confusing. Visualise a group of three people. The first one needs 100 bucks urgently, the second has no money to help but wants to, the third has the 100 and gives it, and it is received gratefully.

The second person is proud of the third as they have done a good deed, but unbeknown to the others the third person grudges handing over the money and doesn't feel the first person deserves it.

So one would expect to see good karma based on what was seen on the surface but in fact what was felt and sent out has a very negative message by the third so providing the first person received gratefully then only the first and second would receive positive karma, the third muddied theirs.

So what kind of message do you think is sent to the Universe when one inadvertently abuses the very powerful message of *ach I will just go with the flow*? Unfortunately and sadly this is all too common. We have all become lazy and undisciplined on many fronts, including with the gift of language, which we take so much for granted.

Our limited use of vocabulary is only serving to confuse our message to the Universe, further adding to the clutter and confusion of *we don't know what we want* and are in fact confusing even when we do know what we want but don't ask for it accurately.

Stability versus Balance

An example I love to quote is as follows. How many times do you hear people say they need to get a more balanced life? Interestingly, when I probe deeper and ask what they actually want, it turns out that it is in fact stability they seek. So they have asked for the complete opposite of balance as balance is the most unstable thing there is. Having achieved balance all it takes is a feather to put it off balance. So how confusing is that when you get the opposite of what you want?

No wonder so many people question the magic of the Universe. Balance is also stationery or stagnant, whereas stability is obtained from motion and the laws of physics clearly demonstrate this. When is a bicycle most stable? When is a plane or a yacht most stable? The answer has to be, when in motion.

This reinforces my earlier point that the power is in the doing. We should not be stationery and stagnant, we need positive forward motion and we need to act on what we want to create. So to obtain stability you must in fact be doing something. However getting back to the point, most people want stability and feel it, but are asking due to their lack of awareness or clarity for the complete opposite and are either neutralising their request or getting the opposite of what they want, once again it's that simple.

Flow is all about motion

So it is most unfortunate when people inadvertently abuse the phrase going with the flow as it is important because so much energy and opportunities are wasted fighting against it. It's far better to be clear when vocalising to the Universe at large and that your thoughts, feelings and words are all as one. It is therefore worthwhile understanding in more detail something like going with the flow.

Flow is all about motion or being fluid and there are many deep and important lessons tied in here. For example, in a storm which tree is likely to be uprooted? Is it the one that stands rigid and fights it, or the one that bends in the wind?

To be rigid may in fact appear strong but the reality, as can be seen in martial arts, is that it can so easily be used against you. To be rigid and inflexible means you are brittle and therefore easily broken.

So being fluid in all that you do and going with the flow of the Universe and life is critically important and will free you up from so much wasted time and energy. Going with the flow can provide you with time and energy so that you can focus and concentrate on what you desire and choose to do in life.

The river of life

Let me paint a picture. Consider life as a giant powerful river surging ever onwards. We are all submerged in that river in life. We then have a choice in that we can either go with the current or against it. Just as in real life, no matter what you choose you will still be swept to your ultimate destination, you can either enjoy the journey or not.

So let's picture what happens when you go against the current, against the flow. Initially you may feel like you are making progress as you appear to be moving through the water, or life, maybe even at speed. However if you take the time to look up at the bank you see that you are in fact being swept along facing backwards.

The fact that you are fighting the current and the flow eventually makes you tired and weary as you fight the same forces in life. Your head drops even lower the more tired you become so you are even less likely to look up at the bank and realise that you are in fact going backwards at all, you are blind and oblivious.

Worse still, as you are facing the wrong way, you never see those rocks or debris and they hit you out of the blue time and time again making you more tired and even wearier. You never ever see where you are going, only where you have been, and it always gets further and further away until eventually you give up and either question what it's all about or drown thinking life was hard and it was hell.

Now imagine the simple action of turning the other way. Wow! Even just by merely floating you will in fact make better progress and preserve your energy, you could in fact stay like that all the way to the final destination and some do indeed choose to coast through life like that. However making some effort is better, for one it helps you to avoid the rocks and debris, which thankfully now will be clearly in your view.

Life is always going to fling rocks and obstacles, obviously its better to avoid them rather than hit them head on. You also have the choice of swimming, which accelerates your journey time and also buys you time to swim to alternative stop offs, have a break, etc. and all these places are in your view and gives you the ability to exercise your free will and make choices.

Before leaving the subject of going with the flow, there is another factor that requires highlighting and it's one of the biggest handicaps flung into the game, and that is FEAR.

Fear is at the root of the majority of problems and it is stopping people from playing the game properly. What do you think would create the most fear - going with the flow where you will have the vision and energy to anticipate and avoid life's obstacles or going against it, head down, weary, and hitting one obstacle after another? So going with the flow has another major benefit, eliminating or minimising fear.

I hear you asking *how do we know which way to face?* Quite simply actually, you feel it and you know it, you probably already do, you just need to ask yourself if your life is energising you or making you weary. Can you see where you are going? Is life easy or incredibly difficult? Is your head up or down? The question for you is, how much do want to change direction? Whilst it's obviously better that you are proactive and choose to change, most don't, and wait on an event that forces them to, or worse still, will waste their whole life. Hopefully I am making that decision and task easier.

I am sure most, if not all, will want to change and will make the effort to go with the flow and learn how to give simple clear heartfelt messages to the Universe. The determined few will do so regardless, and then there will be those that drop off gradually depending on their level of desire.

How much do you want it?

It's like the boy that seeks out the wise old sage in the woods and asks him *is it true that I can create my own reality and get what ever I want?* The sage said *yes, depending on how much you want it.* The boy asks *how much do I need to want it.* The sage said *come with me*, and leads him to the river and submerges him and holds his head under with his hand.

After a few minutes the boy starts to struggle and panic and claws at the Sage's arm. On his last breath the Sage lets him up and states *as much as you wanted that last breath.*

Few want anything that much, most people don't even know what they want, far less focus on what they want. The power of focus cannot be underestimated. Once again the validation for this can be found in the Universe. The sun showers the earth with billions of watts of energy and yet with a hat and some cream you can block it out. However take a few watts of energy and focus it into a laser and you can cut diamonds and cure cancer.

My son and daughter both want a great deal from life however they act in very different manners. Scott appears to have his head in the clouds, a dreamer, and just coasts or sails through life and all good things just land at his feet.

Clare on the other hand seems to have a great work ethic and be very serious and sensible but struggles with a lot of things, the most noticeable being her health.

They are both gifted, in fact very in tune, and Clare regularly displays psychic powers, however on close examination you see that Scott is going with the flow and is generally focussed, as he knows what he wants ultimately, and believes in his dreams and limitless possibilities, and therefore appears to be sailing through life. Don't get me wrong, he has issues and is faced with the temptations and choices all 20 years old face but generally he resists.

Clare would appear to be going against the flow as despite all her hard work and she does work very hard, she never seems to quite get there. In the game we all have freedom of choice so ultimately,

Clare chooses her own way and perhaps she needs more help and guidance as well as experience before making the switch.

I have offered her help and she listens and makes valiant endeavours, but she becomes frustrated. I sincerely hope that reading this book will help her to go with the flow, to identify what she wants and to focus on it as it is also frustrating to watch even though I know we can only take responsibility for our own actions. Something inside tells me that this book will be her catalyst and she will flick that switch and make the change.

I also offered to help Scott, his answer said it all, *no worries dad, I have already programmed success into my head and I will not deviate from that and I can see where I am going.* I still gently present him with options and choices and the possible outcomes of various scenarios but I leave him, like I leave Clare to choose.

Think twice build once

So let me give you some advice on what you should consider before starting your changes, which will help to ensure that you achieve your objectives and increase your chances of success. I am reminded of a phrase I was taught in the construction industry *think twice, and build once.*

My time as a Civil Engineer and then founder and owner of the Ritchie Construction Group has proved invaluable to me, as a great deal of the lessons are transferable into life, as we are constructing and building the life we desire. I have been teased many times by colleagues about my construction stories and I just smile as I watch and wait for the penny to drop and I see them eventually "getting it".

Some of you may feel daunted by the task ahead and it may overwhelm you as you try to take it all in. Once again there are a couple of things that I can share with you that will help you make sense of it all, one from my early construction days, and one recently learned from my business life, so some 25 years experience between those two lessons.

As a young man learning to be a Civil Engineer I obtained the reputation of never saying no and tackling everything, and this later led to me being nicknamed the incredible DIR (my initials David Innes Ritchie). Unfortunately this did not win me many friends, much to my surprise and disquiet, as this was not my intent. I received a call from the then Divisional Director who later went onto become the MD of Amec UK. I was a young trainee and already had older people working under me. He asked if I would go to Niddrie Street Bridge in Paisley Scotland, which was then 9 months behind program, to see if I could help out.

I once again said yes. However on arriving I was given a very cold reception, which threw me off balance and onto my back heels. They did not like the idea of *wonder boy* coming on site. My reputation had been exaggerated and had preceded me.

They dumped a huge pile of drawings on the table in my office and left me to it. I very quickly became overwhelmed and just wanted to leave. At the end of the day I felt physically sick and when the site general foreman came into the office to go home, I ate a huge piece of humble pie and asked sheepishly if he could get the Director on the phone.

He asked me why, and I was honest and told him that I did not believe I could help and had got it wrong by accepting the task and the challenge. After the initial ridiculing (which is typically the Scottish way) he took pity on me, shut the door, and asked me what was on the program for the next day. I told him, *the left bridge abutment*. He asked if I understood what to do and I told him yes. He picked up the drawings specific to the left abutment and put the rest away. He then spent a few hours of his personal time going over it all with me.

I left that night having learned a huge lesson, namely that there is no such thing as a big job, every job is a series of small jobs all linked together. I later created and owned a Construction Group myself having embraced this lesson fully.

So don't let the apparent task ahead of you overwhelm you, just break it down into smaller tasks and take one step at a time.

Baby steps can lead to miracles so taking that first step is the start and it gets easier and easier thereafter.

One of the Key lessons in life is living in the now and this is important here also. There is no point in looking at what needs to be done too far in the future, just focus on what you can do NOW and do it well, this will also help de-stress you and make everything seem easier and manageable.

Capacity Planning

Another transferable lesson is that of *capacity planning.* The best analogy I have seen is that of imagining your business, or in this case a task, or for that matter your life, as a cup.

The first question asked is what size is your cup? Most business owners or bosses actually don't know the answer to this and this is critical, as the philosophy is that you should not move to another cup until you have filled your current cup to a minimum level as it has been demonstrated that if you don't do this and you jump to another cup that is too big and you only have enough to fill it to less than 30% of capacity, then the business or task or whatever will likely fail or require a further injection. You should also not consider moving onto another cup until the existing one is at least 75% full. But how can you do anything if you do not know what size your cup is?

Having established the size of your cup you should also be constantly asking yourself if what you are doing is filling your existing cup or not. Note that this is not a time based thing, but a volume capacity based thing, and therefore the speed you progress is based on how quickly you fill each cup and ensure that the next cup is of a suitable size i.e. 75% of the existing cup must fill more than 30% of the next cup. Hence the reason it is important to only focus on things that are filling your cup.

Know what you are trying to achieve

In order to do this you must know what you are trying to achieve. So let's consider this in general terms, as more detail will follow in the chapters to come. Most people get it wrong by trying to go away from something rather than towards something and this is a hugely important point. For example, I want to give up drinking, I want to quit smoking, I want to lose weight etc. in other words, running away from drinking, smoking or putting on weight, rather than towards your desired goal of a healthier lifestyle and a slimmer figure.

This is a fear based reaction like running away from a bull or lion. How many directions can you go in? Basically there are many directions other than going towards whatever is chasing you, and you do not know what the correct one is, only which one is wrong. However if you are going towards something clear like your desired goal, you only have one choice and it's easy to eliminate all other choices that will not take you there. Once again it is very simple and more on it later.

So in summary, don't be overwhelmed, there is no such thing as a big job, decide where you are going and only make choices that take you there and don't move to the next task until you have sufficiently completed the last one. If you remember that you are immortal and that time is an illusion then you will not panic and will take your time to get it right. That is not saying wait, it is saying take your baby steps to start but start NOW.

Clear the clutter

Before concluding I will keep the construction business theme going. Would you start renovating or reengineering anything without preparing and clearing everything all out first? Likewise, clear your own decks in your life and mind and start with a clean sheet and get rid of the clutter just like you would if you were renovating your house. When completed there will be few of the old pieces that you will want to put back in, you will want to have new, fresh things.

Likewise by clearing out the clutter in your life and mind, you will have space for all the new things and your new positive thinking and you will have removed confusion and clutter. Create new fresh neural pathways eliminating the addiction to the old ways and build new positive healthy ways this time empowered by knowing why and how.

Once again look around you, consider the ancient wisdom of Feng Shui. Is your life cluttered? Are you adding to the confusion? When I got divorced there was a clearing out and a splitting of goods, however I still seemed to have too much. I went a huge stage further when I decided to go and live in Kiev last year and decided to give everything away other than some very small sentimental personal things and clothes.

It was very refreshing and freeing and staggering what I actually had, however 9 months later in Kiev I found I was still gathering and had to give things away again. So we all can gather physical and mental clutter that we don't need. Apply Feng Shui, it works, which should come as no surprise given what I have shared in the Magic of the Universe. Clear that clutter from your mind.

Go with what works for you

Helpful tips are shown at the end as part of the practices and processes however I will say now there is no best way for everyone, and again I will use a business analogy to show this.

In marketing, there are always surveys, for example, one survey I remember was an attempt to determine what the best coffee was and the researchers plotted a graph of the results and chose the one that had the highest peak and that one was chosen as the best. However statistically, this made possibly only 50-60% of the people happy. It was maybe the highest score but 40% were still unhappy. What gave greater customer satisfaction was to offer a number of different options so that people could choose what they liked the most and customer satisfaction in each group then soared to 85% plus.

So there is no such thing as the best of anything for everyone, just what suits you the most. I will show and share what I do and leave you to decide, effectively, opening the door to allow you to look for options. Also, seeking the best invites competition where the Universe works on creation and creativity rather than competition, so instead of looking for what's best in relation to other things, think what mostly fulfils your requirements or the requirements of others, this is non competitive and is instead, highly creative.

So to keep the message clear you must know what you want, know where you are going, focus on it, and live in the now free from doubt and fear, avoid post mortems of the past as you have experienced that already, it's only now that matters. Avoid *what ifs* for the future, once again what purpose does that serve other than to lead to more mixed messages or to cause worry?

Build new neural pathways

Worry is a pointless debilitating energy as you can either do something about the issue or you can't. If you can, do it, as the power is in the doing, or if you can't, let it go or you will create what you fear by giving it energy just by dwelling on it as you send that energy out to the Universe.

Avoid stagnation or ungratefulness, thinking there may be something better out there, the Universe will give you whatever you want, focus on it, if it's not what you want when it arrives, let it go, learn from it, and move on. Avoid the why, why, why or disappointment or blame culture, you chose everything, take responsibility for it, focus on new choices and move on.

Einstein once said that the definition of insanity is to keep doing the same thing over and over again whilst expecting different results. It's amazing how we can advise others but seem to fail miserably when we try to apply that to ourselves so try imagining that your own questions, issues or dilemmas are that of a close friend or loved one, and think how you would advise them. It will suddenly seem oh so clear and simple. Look at how you feel when giving that advice. What do you need to resist in order to create light?

Take control away from the Robot, we have delegated far too much power to it in order to avoid responsibility for the fact that we choose and create our own realities as we are scared of our own power, our endless possibilities.

What if I get it wrong? If so, I have no one to blame but myself. I hope I am giving you the courage to take back the control now that you know how it all works. Trust your gut instinct, we can create both good and bad, if you are open and uncluttered you will feel what is right. Resist the chatter from your mind to do the old things, build new neural pathways and create light.

Playing the Game is about mystery, about discovery, about creation, it's not about being in the know when you know the game is over, because as you will see there is so much you don't know and there are endless possibilities.

The key to the game of life is discovering your own purpose. What do you want to learn? Why did you choose those parents, those friends, those lovers? Go with the flow and enjoy nourishing yourself along the journey.

We are all learning how to play the game and its purpose is to create and experience. Seek out coaches to help you play even better and remember it's not about winning, to seek to win is actually a sign of weakness as it shows that you seek validation, that you need others to tell you who and what you are. Winning is competitive, a man made ego based thing.

The Universe engages with creation not competition, games are about having fun, lightening ones spirit, increasing ones vibration, whilst all the time learning.

Learn to go with the flow.

Above all

remember that positive resistance creates light

Death, the Afterlife and Religion

"There is a finite amount of energy in the Universe at any one time, so nothing can ever be lost or disappear..."

Fear, as I have mentioned before, is a principle obstacle thrown in to make the game more challenging. Unfortunately it has got out of control, out of proportion and out of scale, and impacts and in turn effectively controls far too many lives in a completely negative way, especially in the west or so called developed world.

Whilst there is a place for fear in life as a survival mechanism, a warning or something to make you pay attention, there is a significant difference between the fear that makes you look down as you step on a log to ensure that you do not tread on a rattle snake or when you double check your harness before you jump out of a plane, to the fear that actually STOPS you from doing things and thus makes you avoid engaging with life as you should.

This restrictive type of fear, if it goes unchecked, is able to grow as a result of the mental confusion and clutter that I mentioned in Going with the Flow. Remove the clutter and have a sense of direction in your life and you will minimise fear and start to get it back into proportion, so it's important to deal with any misplaced fears and do what we can to eliminate them from all our lives.

One major fear that is shared globally but with variations depending on ones religion, faith or belief, is that of Death. What happens when I die? This is bound up in the fear of the unknown, the fear of nothingness.

Passing Over

It fascinates me that the most inevitable thing in life that we all face with complete certainty, probably our only guarantee, is what we commonly refer to as death, and yet despite this certainty, or maybe because of it, we try to ignore it, bury it, hide it, anything but look at it and prepare for it or even to celebrate it as many so called primitive cultures do.

The way we use the word death is unfortunate and in my opinion very wrong as we have much better words within our vocabulary, which we do actually use but more often than not when we do use them, we use them unwittingly, once again paying little attention to what we are actually saying. *Passed over*, for example, is by far a more accurate description than the label of *death* we tend to use here in the west and the finality that the word implies.

There is an interesting irony regarding death, which applies whether you believe in the afterlife or eternal life or not, and that is if we treated what we refer to as death with more respect and contemplation, we would in turn respect and value those more that currently share our earthly lives and we would not be crushed with the guilt or remorse saying things like *I wish I had spent more time with them* and *if only...* when someone close to us has passed over.

Before going further I must remind you that all that I say here is my opinion based on my own personal experiences, what I have read, what feels right to me, and ultimately what makes sense to me.

So let's look a bit more closely at the concept of death and consider the Universal Law that there is a finite amount of energy in the Universe at any one time, so nothing can ever be lost or disappear, it just changes state and form and becomes something else, that's all.

What does that mean for us when we die, or anything else for that matter that apparently disappears? Does the change of state result in a loss of memory? The answer is categorically, No! Evidence actually points to the fact that the changed energy or object retains its original memory. Before moving on we should remind ourselves who and what we are.

As stated at the outset, everything in the Universe is quanta, vibration, energy or thinking stuff that is shaped and formed and the more it is shaped the lower its vibration becomes and the more solid it appears. Who am I? I am the person writing this book, I am currently labelled David Innes Ritchie, and these three words are the names given by others to identify the physical body that I currently occupy, the vehicle I use to exist and engage in this earthly plane. No doubt I have had many labels or names throughout my existence.

There is no death for the self

The "I" in you is the person you talk with in your head and this "I" exists on many levels and is capable of transcending or being seen in many dimensions at once, just as quanta is (Doppelgangers springs to mind). Your likeness can appear anywhere and some might call it your spirit, or soul or even your essence, and this energy also has an astral body that the soul or higher self can utilise.

Our higher self exists on a higher vibration plane and ultimately our higher self is the self that is in the likeness of God or Good and is the self that is seeking perfection so that it may return to the source, the centre of all that is Good. Like most hierarchical systems, the higher you rise, the greater the overview of the bigger picture you have.

So back to what happens when we die. The "I" cannot die, there is no death for the self, yes the physical body dies and anyone who has seen a dead body knows that something has gone, something has left, and all that lays there is a carcass, an empty shell, and through the passing of time even that shell reverts back to the source. Just like a dead battery, the energy that made the shell alive has left.

In the case of man, the soul, spirit or essence of "I" departs within the astral body, so if you like the umbilical silver chord that attaches it to the physical body is cut or severed, but it isn't death.

You could in fact liken it to a rebirth, as you will awaken just like a baby on a new adventure and your growth and learning continues, hence the reason we should perhaps celebrate the transformation.

The passing of my father

My father, who was called William Innes Ritchie in this life, decided that after a prolonged period of illness that he was a burden to his wife, my Mother Mary. One day he summoned the energy and got dressed, put his jacket on, which was bizarre given what he was about to do, as he then took his skeletal body out to the garage and hung himself.

I say summoned the energy as his body had faded away to a weight of only 6.5 stone and he barely got one or two hours sleep a day, and even then, only after getting eye drops so he could close his eyes in less pain.

I arrived at my parents' house following phone calls to come home urgently, the calls came from Shona, my wife at the time and also from my neighbour. Shona was one of the first on the scene and kept me updated, unfortunately I was being given the tragic news just as I was boarding a car ferry and therefore could not return immediately and had to do the round trip arriving at my parents a few hours later.

I was taken to see him lying on the garage floor, as my mother and a kind but severely shocked neighbour had lifted him down and the police would not permit the removal of his body at that stage. It was so clear, so very, very clear to me, in fact I had absolutely no doubt whatsoever that all I saw was a shell, a carcass, and my dad had moved on.

I bent down, kissed the shell on the forehead, and wished my father well on his new journey. This was my first direct experience of a dead person and it served to validate, reinforce and crystallise my beliefs.

A couple of nights later my father joined me in a dream and he was very angry, which totally surprised me, and I asked him why he was getting at me. He answered that he was frustrated as he only had a short time, he stated 48 hours, and he now had to move on. We hugged and that was that. Thankfully my dad has often visited me in my dreams since then and I still get chastised from time to time.

I did a lot of my grieving for my father later on in a somewhat spontaneous fashion and generally at the strangest of times over the years. At the time of his departure I think I convinced myself that as the eldest, especially as a formidable character, I was expected to be strong and that I should be strong for everyone else.

However I also had another reason and that was I realised that my grieving would mostly be selfish as it would mean I did not want what my dad wanted for himself and I would be thinking of me not him. I realised that I should celebrate his life and not mourn his loss but still acknowledge the grief of missing him.

This was intuitive to me at the time and I later learned that it is by far the best thing you can do for a departed loved one. Respect their passing, celebrate their life and let them be free to enjoy their new journey as you get on and enjoy yours, otherwise you can hold them back with your longing and keep them in a transitional space. However, given there is no concept of time I believe this to be more of an inconvenience and frustration than anything else.

I also believe they can see you at anytime in an instant just by thinking about you and the higher your vibration and the lighter your spirit then the more likely this will be to happen as they will struggle with lower negative vibrations. This does not mean forget them, far from it, love them and do what you know they would want you to do, make them proud.

Let me expand on this for a moment. When I say *do what you know they would want you to do*, I am not referring to some obligation that you feel you may be obliged to fulfil, what I mean is live your life to the fullest as this is what they would want you to do. Having passed over, things are much clearer to them now, and all they would want is for you to live your life and not hold them back or yourself. Celebrate their existence and make them proud by being the best you can be.

I acknowledge that this is easy to say, and in doing so, I consider a number of things. The passing of a child is without doubt a tragedy and one of the worst experiences any parent would ever have to go through and it must feel so terribly wrong and unjust. Having never directly experienced this, I can do little or nothing to ease that pain, other than to help you try and understand and process the grief and maybe help you to accept that they have not died in the pure sense of the word, they have simply moved ahead of you, and in the greater scheme of things will be together with you again one day in the twinkling of an eye, especially for them.

On the passing of my father I apologised to many who I had previously paid condolences to as I had said the words of comfort to them but only with the passing of my own father did I feel the emotions, the pain, the void, and in turn come to understand what they had felt, again highlighting the importance of experience in life. I am reminded of a story.

The story of the mustard seed

A distraught and grieving mother arrived at the home of a wise old sage with a dead baby in her arms and she cried *is it true that you can bring my child back to life?* The sage replied *yes*, so she said *what must I do, I will do anything?* He told her to bring him some mustard seed from a household that has not been touched by death. *Is that all?* She said. *Yes* was the reply *that's all*.

She ran from door to door, from house to house, and slowly but surely she realised that each and every one of us are all touched by death, it is the way of the Universe, and she settled down to grieve for the loss of her child.

Near death experience

Some people have a head start over the rest of us by experiencing death temporarily or by having a near death experience. Most of these who have recounted their experiences share the feeling of returning to the light, to something that they had forgotten about, and to having a feeling of pure bliss. They can accurately describe what the doctors and nurses were saying after being pronounced dead and blind people have even been able to describe what the people were wearing, including the colours. Most talk of loved ones waiting on them to guide them through.

There are also sceptics who roll out arguments to prove, in their opinion, that this state can be replicated psychologically and that there are scientific reasons that explain it all, and will even proclaim that when we die that is it, NOTHINGNESS.

Are these the people who are so busy looking at the spot on the knee of the fly that they have forgotten that it is a fly they are looking at? Can they not see the bigger picture? Because even if that were true, that there really is nothing after death, can you show me just one of those very self same people who live their life as if this is all there is? I doubt it.

I doubt that they are wearing the funeral directors watch that is ticking backwards to the time of their passing and are therefore living every moment to the full. Why not? Because at a deep level they feel immortal, that they have time.

Life after death

As a young guy, I was given a book by a work colleague Tony O'Donnell, it was called "Mysteries" and the author was Colin Wilson. I was fascinated as it touched on a lot of things within what is generally labelled the paranormal, some of which I had experienced personally, so it gave me great comfort to read about the experiences of others.

Once again, it is clearly an advantage when you have actually experienced them yourself as it is easier to accept certain things, which reinforces why we are on this earthly plane, to experience things first hand about cause and effect, action and reaction.

I was so taken by Colin Wilson's writing that I searched out much of his work and they became like comfort blankets to me. He was commissioned to write a book on the Occult and in researching the subject he had become totally and utterly convinced that amongst other things, there is existence after death. His book "Beyond the Occult" was the culmination of 20 years research where he states convincingly that the evidence is overwhelming in favour of other dimensions, spirits, and life after what we call death.

I owe Colin Wilson a great deal and I intend to share this book with him. He inspired me, and ironically, the more I read the more I wanted to write something like this book here, a simplified guide if you like, something short and straightforward to act as a stepping stone to the more in-depth writers such as Colin Wilson.

There are also a number of mainstream mediums, psychics and clairvoyants who defy the sceptics such as the likes of Jonathon Edwards, Silvia Brown, Colin Fry, and Gordon Smith to name a few. All of them clearly demonstrate that there is something real and more and that death is not nothingness, it's not black, it's merely a change of state.

Contact beyond the grave

Out of curiosity I recently went along to one of Colin Fry's shows in the Edinburgh Playhouse. It was full with 3000 people in attendance, and he had every single one of us laughing and crying, we were amazed.

He stated at the beginning that he sympathised with those in the audience that were currently grieving, but he insisted that we must all lift our spirits as negative emotions are at such a low vibration it makes it all but impossible for anyone to get through as it is difficult enough for the spirit to lower its vibration enough to communicate with those who are already happy and vibrating at a higher level.

If I needed convinced, which I did not, it would have been that night. My daughter held my hand throughout, we laughed, we cried, we shared in the amazing energy of the evening. She was nervous of going along and when I asked her why she said *well I am still young, I do not know that many dead people* and l laughed at the irony. I would like to share with you one of the readings that night.

A grandmother came through to her granddaughter and Colin gave a very accurate description of her and it was very evident from the Granddaughter's body language and uncontrollable bursts of laughter that Colin was talking with what represented the Granddaughter's Grandmother. He said that her Grandmother no longer visited her mother as she was always so negative. The granddaughter confirmed that this was the current state of her mother's mood.

The Grandmother also asked that a message be passed onto the mother, which was to give herself a shake, and if she hadn't changed her mood by the time she passed over not to come looking for her. At the last moment the Grandmother (through Colin) described accurately not only her funeral and questioned the lack of flowers, but also her grave. She asked a favour, that her vase be cemented down as the visitors to the next graves kept stealing it. The Granddaughter laughed knowingly and announced that the neighbouring graves were that of her Grandmother's sisters.

I have certainly had my own experiences and wonder how many others have their own stories that they could tell? I would imagine that every household in the land contains someone who has something to say. No, we don't die, we pass over and we go back to where we came from, where we belong, and the desire to do so is perhaps more deep-rooted than we realize.

How do we know all this about the other side, the after life, the eternal life? It is ancient wisdom after all so the information is already here and we are simply reminded of it by many sources, teachers from ancient times, near death experiences or those that have died briefly, mediums, mystics, clairvoyants, even you and me when we look deeply into our subconscious minds for the answers. All of these sources help to build up a picture that is all but impossible to deny other than by those clearly in denial.

Visitations

I am currently writing this section of the book in CA, USA and I would like to share a story with you that happened just before I left Scotland in December last year. I was staying at my mother's house for a few weeks and whilst I was there, my Daughter Clare along with her son, my Grandson Aidan who is two years old, came to visit us one night.

Aidan needed the toilet and Clare went to take him, but he stopped dead, (forgive the pun) at the bathroom door, and when Clare asked what was wrong he replied *I am not going in until the man goes away.* Clare asked *what man Aidan, what is the man doing,* to see if it was just his imagination and Aidan replied *he is fixing the doors.*

My Dad was constantly doing things around the house so when I heard this taking place I shouted through to Aidan *what's the man's name?* Aidan replied *Willie*, which as I stated earlier, was my father's name, he was called Bill and Handsome Willie. Aidan was born 4 years after my father had passed over. Aidan informs us that Willie often visits him in his own bedroom at home and later when he was shown pictures of my dad by Clare, he confirmed it was Willie.

I have experienced a number of things with Clare. When she was only three she was sitting at the bottom of the stairs crying and when I asked why she was crying, she said it wasn't her that was crying it was her Auntie Margaret. Just at that point her aunt arrived and announced that she had just been diagnosed with cancer.

Then again on another night I was wakened by a loud crash. The painting above the fire place had fallen down and I went to check that the kids had not been wakened by it only to find that Clare was being sick in her sleep and could have choked on it if I had not gone through and in turn been wakened myself by the picture inexplicably falling down. Some people might be afraid if they encounter experiences like this, but why?

There is nothing to fear but fear itself

We should try to eliminate restricting FEAR and particularly fear of DEATH as it does not exist, it is an Illusion. Now, if you can accept and embrace this, and combine this information with that in the previous chapter, what are the implications?

You will have virtually eliminated negative fear. How powerful is that? How different is your life going to be without disabling fear, knowing that there is nothing to fear but fear itself? Ironically, in reality, deep down, man does not fear how weak he is, but in fact how powerful he is, and what man truly struggles with is taking responsibility for this and for what he has created and continues to create.

So what happens when we pass over? Forgive me but it is not easy for me to express what I see in my minds eye and sense and understand to be the case. I also feel somewhat embarrassed to acknowledge that in the past I have wanted to die or more accurately wanted to pass over and was preoccupied with killing myself for such a large period of my life.

Now after years of attending psychologists off and on, and receiving self help and guidance from astrology and spiritualists, I realise the following as a personal truth for me.

I did not wish to die or kill myself, I wished to destroy or remove an aspect of myself that I did not like and I also wanted to return to where I knew I belonged.

All I can do is share with you what I have learned and in turn what makes sense to me and hope it is helpful for you too.

Different levels of existence

At the centre of everything is what we have called God, the core, the source, the light, and as we move away from the core we have different levels differentiated by variances in vibration and the purity of the light until we arrive at this level that we currently inhabit, the solid lowest vibration level i.e. the earthly plane.

This earthly plane was created to experiment, to test and to show what happens with undisciplined ideas and to feel, to experience the emotions associated with it, not as a punishment or anything negative but in a creative fashion. However we retain free will and are therefore permitted to make and experience our mistakes, the key always is experience.

When we leave the physical realm we pass to the astral realm where unlike the physical realm there is no time and our thoughts and desires are created and manifested instantly. The fact that there is no time in the other realms explains a number of things such as why when people return from temporary death or near death and say their life flashed before them in a second.

Well as there was no time it was as if it was being played back and they were recalling it all in order to see if they had learned what they had originally chosen to learn.

Every level you move up is at a higher vibratory plane and as such, things appear more real, more colourful, and you can replicate all that you had on this plane if that is what you desire to do. Like for like is attracted together so you will be surrounded by those of similar vibratory levels and desires i.e. birds of a feather flock together.

Is there a heaven? Not as such, there is the core, the source, good, but you have many levels and possibly many reincarnations to go through first before reaching that level.

Do not feel disheartened if you struggle to grasp all this, all will become clearer as you rise from level to level, and given that we are currently on the lowest level, it is no wonder that we struggle to understand it all. Likewise, is there a hell? Not as such either, the same rule applies, as above so below.

In both cases you create your own reality on the astral plane, just as you do on the earthly plane, but the difference is it happens in an instant and there is no time. Those familiar with computers will get a glimpse of this, jumping from one section of a hard drive to another in an instant, bringing up videos of you as a child, as an adult and so on.

Our sleep and dream time also gives us a great insight into what's possible as you flit from one reality to another in your dreams whilst still retaining the memory of your waking life.

However there is a cautionary note as there nearly always is, and that is your beliefs and actions on the earthly plane will determine what you experience on the next plane, as Karma works on all planes. And so you will create a reality for yourself in line with your beliefs.

If you are a religious zealot you will be surrounded by religious zealots, a thief, by thieves, murderers by murderers, liars by liars and so on, so if you like it is possible to create your own version of hell on earth. Likewise with heaven or your version of whatever you think it is.

And there you will remain, in that timeless zone, until either helped or until you come to the realisation that you wish to change and grow and back you will come to learn your lessons on this plane by choosing a certain path and who you will interact with on that path. It certainly does sound very much like a game, the ultimate game, and therefore the rules reflect this.

Films like the Matrix touch upon the possibilities of such things and allow ones imagination to grasp the potential. The film Groundhog Day also is a play on the rules of reincarnation as back you come until you get it right and you play out certain roles, all complicated by the fact that the others in the game also have free will.

Death, the Afterlife and Religion

The character in Groundhog Day had the advantage of recall so knew what he wanted to achieve. We too can tap back into this and in doing so make the game easier to play and increase the likelihood of a successful outcome.

There are different levels of help available all in line with what we have heard in the ancient teachings. Energy beings from all over the Universe ranging from fairy tale creatures to angels and superior beings whose intellect is as far above ours as ours is above an insect, but we should never forget that we are all connected.

Everything we have dreamt, thought about, and created, exists because it was shaped by thought, which is why money has been given disproportionate importance and energy, so many people have focussed upon it. There is no food on the astral plane. There is no need for it as we have no body in the sense that we consider it. This for me answers a lot of the confusion over the dilemmas we face on this plane regarding food stuff.

Some people are vegetarians, either because of a health choice or because they do not wish to see animals treated in such a manner. Science has proven that plants too have feelings of sort. In one experiment some plants were connected to a lie detector machine and registered a reading when a person who had destroyed a fellow plant entered a room, they "recognised" him. So where do we draw the line? More of this in a later chapter but it's good to know that it is no longer an issue in the next realm as we no longer need to consume. It also reinforces the importance of the soul or spirit, the source of our desires and thoughts, the core of whether we are our best friend or own worst enemy.

I have heard that those who suffer from weight issues do so as they wish to protect their soul from the cruelties of the world by creating a protective shield if you like. This certainly adds a new and interesting dimension to the whole dieting fad i.e. deal with the soul or the spirit first, along with the desires and the thoughts and watch the shield fall away.

Everything that has happened and is going to happen is all recorded in what is called the Akashic library, and this is the culmination of all our creations. There is help, as mentioned before, and councils, guides, etc. all focused on evolving and creating.

Our ultimate higher self, the ultimate "I" is asexual, neither male nor female, and like all things in creation, contains aspects of both male and female to make the whole. There is obviously no reproduction and no sex in the physical sense however one can merge energies to achieve that sense of climax and orgasm.

I mentioned in a previous section that we should never complain about where we are at in life as we chose it, likewise in the spiritual plane. If you like we sit down with who we elect to be our spirit guide and map out the path we wish to follow in the next life in order to learn the lessons we require for growth.

Astrology

The Universe could be likened to a giant computer, just like in the matrix, that runs the selected programs. Nothing can be left to chance as otherwise the Universe would be in chaos and it clearly has order to it. Astrology taps into this order.

Astrology if you like proves that there is not only a super computer, the ultimate computer, but also the ultimate programmer who wrote the programs. Astrology works as there has to be some order to things, so if we are born in a certain place at a certain time then a particular program is run. The movements of the planets impact on the energy, which in turn influences the likelihood of events, hence the reason astrology can say you are likely to behave in a certain way.

Once again I have direct experience of astrology and therefore in turn validation of how amazing and true astrology can be. What's even more amazing to me is who created astrology in the first instance and when? The reason I sow this seed is to reaffirm that so called death cannot be nothingness, as the evidence to prove otherwise is overwhelming and all around us if we will only open our eyes and see.

Once we return to earth with the path of our choice, family of our choice, and everything else we choose, the spirit guides watch over to assist where possible. This isn't to help us avoid misfortune but to ensure that the lessons we need to learn are learned as there is no benefit in avoiding the lesson as karma will force it to be repeated.

Religion

I will leave this topic at this, as the point of the book is to whet ones appetite and sow seeds, and there are many books and people out there who can go into this matter in much greater detail and you can choose what you want to believe. Before departing completely, I must touch on a subject matter that is closely related and intertwined with death, and that is religion.

The word fear once again immediately comes to mind and whilst I cannot boast to know all religions, I can say without fear of contradiction that most eventually become fear based in order to retain power and control over others, which is very sad indeed, as it would appear that most religions start out with a very different intent.

There are a number of issues that I truly struggle with when it comes to organised religions. As I stated already, I do believe that at the core of all of them is the best of intention and an appreciation and acknowledgement that there is something bigger and better out there.

There are billions who take comfort from their religion and provided that this is not abused, that is fantastic. Unfortunately, individuals often become corrupted after a while, mainly because they shift from the creative i.e. the creation of good, love and light, to the competitive and my God is better than your God and my religion is right and yours is wrong and so on.

I struggle when I see churches owning billions and billions of assets and preach that we should look after the poor but focus themselves on becoming wealthier and not sharing. Or playing the opposite side, they often play the abstinence card saying that poverty and chastity is the answer and this in my opinion is not strictly true, it is a deception, and doesn't ultimately create a better world for the family of man.

There are also irresponsible individuals, who unfortunately exist in all walks of life, but when exposed within a religion the significance or importance of their errors are magnified because the religions have set themselves up to be better, to lead the way so to speak, and therefore the expectations are greater.

Are we only trying to make ourselves feel better by judging them as we have delegated our responsibility onto others?

I mostly struggle with the fact that so many organised Religions play on fear and insecurity and people's resistance to take responsibility for how powerful they are. People want a father, a mother or big brother to fix it for them and religion fills this void and plays this role. One should not blame religion *per se* as it is man made and we, *en masse,* chose to endorse it and allow it to happen.

It can be a challenge to find a positive argument when we look at history, the wars, the greed, the control, all done in the name of one religion or another. As one religion obtained dominance over another they would take what they liked and wanted from the old religion, sometimes just to ensure compliance in the merger, and then would demonize what they did not want.

So called civilized man would explore and conquer country and nation, taking their religion with them and forcing it upon the so called natives, the so called uncivilized. Yet these ancient civilizations had universal knowledge, faith, and philosophies that were shared around the world despite the lack of transport or books, an ancient wisdom that science is only validating now.

Yes there have been and will continue to be great teachers and coaches who share the universal rules, however, whilst it appeared to prove useful to write these teachings down when writing was created, many of these books were awarded mystical powers by the religious leaders who not only used them to control the masses but also chose and censored the content.

Such travesties and untruths are now being exposed for what they are. Man seems to choose to forget that all the great books were written by man and not only were they censored but more often than not, poorly translated. But note, I say GREAT BOOKS, as that is what they are, they have truth and guidance within them and no one can deny that, it's how this "truth" is applied or interpreted that causes the issues.

Religion, by its very existence, proves in a way that we recognise there is something more or other-worldly. I don't believe that the bible and other great books are in any way fraudulent as some would try to say. We must remember that they are written by MAN and as man is far from perfect, the books can be tainted in man's attempt to make them more palatable by humanising and possibly politicising them. The end result is that so many people end up focussing on the picture that is painted and forget the original message.

What is the message?

In the main, all religions have similar messages of hope and encouragement, wisdom and guidance that really help people cope with life and it is therefore such a shame when these same messages are distorted or misinterpreted and used for personal gain or to force the aims of the religion itself on others. Tolerance is the key here but so many people don't seem to know what that means.

Naturally, many people are defensive when it comes to the subject of religion but what really matters is the original or core message or intent, the words between the words, which is remarkably similar in all religions. Basically, it is the attempt to live life in such a way that it makes each man, woman and child a better person and to live without fear and in harmony with others to enhance the quality of life for all.

Regardless of how a particular religion tells its own story, it is this that makes the difference and if we could all abide by the original messages of love and goodness in our daily lives, we would all be able to respect one another's right to choose what we want to believe and which religion we wish to follow.

Recently I have had two women in my life who in their own ways were influenced by religious teachings and it is worth mentioning because of their diversity, and also because of the good that was obtained.

Irina is Ukrainian and comes from a communist background where religion was forced underground, which ironically gave it even more mystical powers and a devoted following. Irina reads the Russian Orthodox Bible most nights and keeps it by her bedside. I asked her why she reads the bible and she answered *it's a good book with interesting stories and provides wise guidance*.

The other woman was Fay from London. Fay had been introduced to the Jehovah Witness religion by her father who had turned to it later in his life. Fay also read the bible regularly, in this case the Jehovah's Witness version. She has more opinionated views but also stated that when she studied and practiced what she read her life improved for the better. Interestingly for me is that whilst very different people and coming from vastly different cultures they actually took the time to read the bible and both got something positive from it albeit from different versions.

Few people actually ever read their bibles from their chosen religions and choose to accept others interpretations and it is even rarer that people read the bibles from other religions, and yet they still feel qualified to judge and criticise.

What is the correct version of the bible? Who knows, perhaps it's hidden away from us or the answers lie in the dead sea scrolls, for me its irrelevant, and what matters is to remind ourselves what the fundamental message running through them all is, and that is to teach us all how to grow and return to the light, to the source, to God.

How can any sensible intelligent person take a deity such as God (regardless of what religion one follows) who represents all that is good, all that has ever been and created, all that we know and are dazzled by in this magical Universe, whose intellect and knowledge is so far beyond our comprehension, and then try and justify their greed, ignorance and fears by saying its god's will and furthermore, that my religion is right and yours is wrong. It's nonsense beyond all

Death, the Afterlife and Religion

nonsense. The pure act of believing in God means that you would not judge and would in turn help, assist and love your fellow man.

We create our own realities and it is our fear of taking responsibility for our own actions that causes people to project this onto religion and in doing so, distort and poison the truth and message behind all religions. It is time people woke up and accepted this and stopped blaming someone else's God.

The ultimate irony

The purpose of life, the point of the game is to learn, to expose, to experience, and to grow, and it all makes sense if we accept that we are immortal and don't die, we just change, and this is our virtual reality game.

We, as a whole, are the creators of tragedy, loss, famine and misfortune, and we CHOOSE to continue to create this even though there is enough money in the world so to speak for everyone to live a comfortable life.

This brings me nicely to a universal law and the root of why most organized religions fall down and that is that we cannot influence the free will of another. It is their gift, and is an essential part of playing the game, the freedom of choice to choose. But so many religions try to force and control, rather than to teach and lead by example, and allow people to choose for themselves.

Am I against any religion? Absolutely not! I am against what it appears to have become and I am against how it has been corrupted and I am against how it is used as a shield to cover wrong doing. I have had a number of bad experiences with religious people but equally I have had some very good ones.

I once built a chapel for a catholic organisation, and on completion they refused to pay for the extras. The priest in charge said *sue us if you can find out who to sue*, and he was right, it was virtually impossible to sue the Catholic Church. In this case it was the individual and not the religion but he used the privilege of the religion. I embrace everything that has a wish to improve the Universe that we live within, and people's faith is a good thing, as long as it's not manipulated or abused.

To have faith in something intangible is a great step forward to grasping the full realities of the Universe. Religion is its own worst enemy, its fear of change, its avoidance of creation, has in the main caused it to stagnate and lose touch and get out of tune with the Universe and has resulted in an ageing diminishing congregation who are there more out of fear and robotic habit than out of love and belief.

I appreciate that this is a generalisation and is purely based on my own opinion and experience. The general frustration that surrounds all this has caused splinter and radical groups to form, some with the best of intent, but they have focused on selected sections rather than on developing a cohesive whole or they are driven out of political hate and rarely out of love and creation.

So called civilisation has contributed greatly to the demise of organised religion, not just because of the leaning towards materialism but also the fragmentation of the family unit and communication which was accelerated by the industrial revolution making people more isolated.

The digital revolution has actually further encouraged isolation but things are changing and it will not take much to use these self same mediums, technologies and religions, to create a better environment for us all. Just like the shaman, the religious leaders can help their people see the reality, the possibilities, but only when they have the courage to do so.

Here is the ultimate irony. We are all as one, we are all energy beings, all connected, everyone is a part of everyone else, if you see something that you don't like in others, it's a reflection of you. Fundamentally, all people are good, are in search of happiness, to return to the source, and are driven by desire and imagination.

So love your fellow man or women as they are all part of you and you them. Embrace their teachings and their respective religions. Learn what you can, question why you feel the way you do, and resist the temptation to tarnish your beliefs and your religion by becoming intolerant and judging others. Above all remember that positive resistance creates light.

Act now, as Good really does come to those that make the effort to help themselves

Life and Abundance and Success

"Learning the difference between need and want is essential, in fact critical, as it is at the root of all our emotional and in turn psychological problems"

We now know that positive resistance creates light, and taking aside that we are all connected in a universal sense at a molecular level, and by desire and imagination, we also share a common search for happiness.

Happiness has unfortunately been confused with gaining wealth and possessions and so on. The reality is that to be happy one just needs to think happy thoughts, and given the fact that thoughts influence every aspect of our lives and our Universe, then this has to be a valid and accurate statement. I have practiced and dwelled on this and yes I can now flip to being in a happy state by suggestion alone.

Some of you may be able to instantly accept this and jump straight onto it, unfortunately most wont, and therefore there is a process that we must go through to help you reach that stage and by taking baby steps to begin with, you can move towards your own personal miracle.

The idea of jumping straight to the miracle may have an appeal but the thought of leaping will overwhelm most and to a certain extent that is acceptable and is a built in safety mechanism to protect you. You would not wish to try a ski jump without learning the basics and practising and progressing at your own pace until you feel able and are encouraged to do it. So we must positively resist the restrictive, disabling fear that is deluding you to stay within your comfort zone and help you to keep pushing and moving forward.

Our comfort zones are horrible, stagnant, smelly places to be, but we cannot see it whilst within those comfort zones, we can only see it when looking back, and when you do, you will be aghast that you accepted that state.

Do you know what you want?

In this section I am going to share with you in as simplistic terms as I can, how you can achieve, create and manifest whatever you want. In other words, show you how to apply the rules and play the game to its fullest extent.

Let's begin by considering a very common fact, and that is that the vast majority of people do not know what it is they want. Do you? Yes, you may make general sweeping statements like *I want to be happy* and *I want to be rich*, but what does that actually mean? What in fact are you asking for? You may struggle with this initially yourself, but do a test, ask friends and loved ones what they really want. I am sure that most, as I say, will struggle to answer. There are a couple of issues with this.

We have discussed that you can create your own reality and the Universe delivers whatever you ask for without question or hesitation. So if you don't know what you want, then it comes as little surprise that you will not get what you want. You will in turn get what you need and probably a lot of what you don't want. You are also giving a message to the Universe that *wanting* is what you want so you will be kept wanting.

Establishing what you want and why in the first place is critically important, and then you must focus on that, and that alone will create it in your life.

I am reminded of the phrase be careful of what you wish for as it will come true. You ask for a beautiful woman and she arrives into your life but you forgot to specify that she should love you and not another. So it's important to think it all through first.

Write it down, there is a magic in that action alone. Write down what you want or should I say think you want. I have stated that everything is possible and explained why in the magic of the Universe so let's look at what will make you happy, what will fulfil you and sustain you.

Abundance

The Universe has an abundance of everything we need and ever wanted, it's all there to be manifested. You just need to believe it and you will see it, just like the story about the Native American Indians who it was said couldn't see the ships when Columbus arrived; you have just been programmed not to see it.

What is Abundance? Abundance is to have more than you need it's that simple, not more than you want, but more than you need.

Everyone's needs are different, as are our wants, but learning the difference between need and want is essential, in fact critical, as it is at the root of all our emotional, and in turn psychological problems. For example, a person living in the heart of a city doesn't necessarily need a car but someone living in a rural area does, and yet the city dweller may want a car and stress over what particular car to buy and where they can park it safely.

Sadly our conditioning has been to focus on what we do not have rather than what we have. We have a misplaced value on objects and in turn processes that we have been led to believe are required in order to achieve the possession of these objects.

I mentioned Warren Buffett earlier, one of the richest men in the world. Despite his enormous wealth, he lives in a modest house and drives himself to work in his own modest car and he doesn't have any security guards. I use the word modest in that what he has is modest in relation to the size of his wealth.

He comes across as warm, happy, wise and humble. He certainly seems to have got things in perspective and chooses not to pursue the glamorous life that he could more than afford and has also given a large part of his fortune away.

Now let me reinforce something here and now, I am not against anyone having everything and anything they want as there is sufficient abundance in the Universe to allow this to happen, what I want is to help you understand the difference between need and want so that you do not waste energy pursuing an illusion, the illusion that it will make you happy by possessing it.

The challenge of the game is that most will continue to pursue the illusion as most will need to experience it before they accept and understand this. But it would be wrong of me not to share what I have learned, and then you can be free to choose.

The world as we know it has become increasingly materialistic and uses this as a measure of success, but, and it is a big but, most people who are successful as measured on the materialistic level are not happy. Also the desire for material success is at the root of most problems ranging from a mild feeling of inadequacy, because you don't have what you see others as having, which may lead to dishonesty and even crime, and at the other extreme a pathological desire for power and money, which can ultimately lead to murder, death and war.

This is played out for all to see on the world stage. The tension continues as the world watches those who have tentatively learned from their mistakes try and stop those emerging countries from doing the same thing. If this is genuine then it is a great thing and for the good of all, helping others learn from costly mistakes.

Unfortunately, the manner in which they generally endeavour to do this creates animosity as they project that it is more to do with sustaining or bettering their own materialistic position than as a genuine gesture to help the other country or the planet as a whole.

A few words on ownership

Things would be so different if we all understood the difference between need and want and the negative power that has been placed on material possessions, money being the biggest of all.

I am not in any way going to try to stop you from achieving what you want, in fact I am going to help you accelerate it and create more than you dreamed possible. Most importantly, I am going to show you how to be happy whilst doing so and contribute to the positive development of mankind as a result. The principle difference is going to be a shift in the non material sense as it will be your state of mind, your thought process will change, not the amount of your so called possessions or assets.

I say "*so called*" for a number of reasons. The fact is that you cannot take one material thing with you when you pass on, that is an indisputable truth, so how can you say you own something? The borders of countries change, land masses change, as nature, man and his wars does its stuff in both cases. Does saying that you own something make it yours? You cannot pass it onto your family if it has been wiped out or transferred to another country.

Let's simplify it. If I approach you with a gun and take your Rolex, will it magic itself back to you because you allegedly owned it? Of course not, you don't own anything and the real danger in believing that you own something is that it starts to own you, you have given up your power, your magic of creation, to an inanimate lifeless object. Not only that, you may suffer stress and make yourself ill over trying to keep it rather than using your gift, your magic, to create more and more for you and your family.

So the shift is a thought shift. I am not asking you to give up anything other than a controlling and restrictive thought and to replace it with a positive thought that helps you to realise no one actually owns anything. Ownership or the illusion of ownership is a man made concept and its creation has led to a desire to control, mainly out of fear and insecurity.

You hear the words but are you registering? Most people who have achieved material success are not happy. Look at the media, the press, and look at your friends, the evidence is all around you. What makes you think you would be any different? The fact is you won't, until you change your thinking. So what is important?

Money, Money, Money

I flew back to Scotland to finish the book with JJ and my son Scott came to visit me and we walked down the beach to the point at Findhorn where we had scattered my fathers ashes, his favourite place and one of ours too. We were watching the waves crash in and were covering many subjects mainly triggered by memories of all those we have stood there with over the years and we got onto the subject of coastal erosion and global warming.

I recommended that he watch the movie "An inconvenient truth" so that he could get an overview and then form his own opinions. I also pointed out that we are always only four days away from complete energy and fuel shut down should a major event occur. He was shocked by this and said *what bloody use will money be then*?

For me it was a great example of how worthless money is and I am glad that it helped him ground himself and get things into perspective. Is it going to stop him pursuing his dreams? No! He has just got things into perspective.

The really important things in life have got to be health, loving relationships, and the free will to create what we desire. So like me, Scott now thinks about what he needs and then accepts that his wants are just wants and if he gets them great, but equally if he does not he wont stress over it as he has more than he needs. The key is that he will still strive like I do for my wants, the only change is in perspective and we have not given away our power or magic.

Imagine for a moment that you have £10 million in the bank. I love watching the expressions on peoples faces change and a smile appear when they start to contemplate that fact. This demonstrates a couple of things. That happiness is a state of mind, as the thought alone changed them, and that so much emotional importance is placed on having money. I then ask what would you do if you had that kind of money, how would you live your life differently?

After the usual buy a house, new cars, presents, holidays, etc. and you ask what then? You see them reflect and say that they would spend their time doing what they enjoy doing. Invariably, the answers are something like fishing, painting, sailing, gardening, enjoying nature and such like.

I then hit them with the killer blow that jolts them into realising what they really want and ask them *why can't you do that now?* As in practically all cases, nothing they mentioned required the vast sums of money they thought they required.

There are also those that can't even imagine that they would have 10 million, not because they don't desire it, but because they don't believe they deserve it. These people are worse off as they have a double negative as they not only have self doubt that tells the Universe that they don't deserve anything, they also have a desire for an illusion that makes them unhappy because they don't have it.

What it means to be Truly Rich

The good news is we all deserve to be rich and wealthy and can be, when we consider my definition of rich. I don't know about you but *rich* is a wonderful word that encompasses much more than just money in ones mind, even more powerful than wealthy. To be truly rich is to have more than you need and to have the health to enjoy it and to experience love and happiness in life and to be open and non-judgemental to all that surrounds us and touches us.

That is Truly Rich, and I intend to do all I can to help ensure that you become Truly Rich. I hope that you already feel that warm glow building within you just reading those magic words Truly Rich.

There is little doubt that by making the thought shift, that change of state of mind, and recognising the difference between need and want, is paramount to ensuring that you successfully play the game and achieve all you desire and join the others who are making the decision to become Truly Rich.

When you are rich, Truly Rich, everything in life improves and becomes easier. It is easier to develop new and fulfilling relationships. You give more, not just in a material sense but of yourself. You can lead by example and the law of attraction means that you will attract like minded people and so it will grow and grow

Life and Abundance and Success

as if by magic. So becoming Truly Rich encompasses many things, it's a holistic approach which all starts from within in that you create who you are by what you think.

Learn the difference between need and want

I have heard and use the terms *you are what you eat,* and *a healthy body leads to a healthy mind,* and yes there is a correlation and an element of truth to these statements, but the fact is that healthy thoughts are what matters first and foremost. So what do we need versus what do we want?

I over simplify this sometimes when I speak with people and state that I recognise that I need very little but want a great deal and that I also accept that if my needs are fulfilled then I will not be overly concerned about not receiving my wants.

This is an accurate statement but has one fundamental flaw, it's a bit like putting the cart before the horse, and that is, I missed out a very key element, which is that I personally have already spent some focused time establishing what I need and what I want and you need to do the same.

Our needs can be split into a number of subsections. We have needs to exist and survive within the environment that we have chosen, I say chosen as it may be a location that you chose because of work or it may be in a spiritual context in order to pay some karmic debt or lesson.

In other words there will be basic needs required just to live, like food, shelter and safety. We then have our spiritual needs and what lessons we need to learn, and this will encompass a more readily accepted aspect of emotional needs through relationships for example.

The exercises at the end of the book help you establish the difference between your needs and wants and will help you prepare what I call MY REALITY sheet which I have shared later in the chapter.

Be specific about what you want

I mentioned that all that matters is NOW and it is so very important to grasp and understand that. To become TRULY RICH you must act NOW as if you are already TRULY RICH, you must believe NOW that you are TRULY RICH and never fall into the all too common traps that I will highlight below.

Remember the Universe has been designed to ensure that creation continues and it delivers exactly what you ask for without question every time, it does not question or judge, it just delivers.

It doesn't matter what has gone before other than you have old neural networks that you will have to undo and you should positively resist the withdrawal symptoms that will go along with that. The desire and courage associated with knowingly and lovingly heading in the direction of your own choosing will overcome all of this.

Believe me, trust me and most of all believe in you and trust in yourself. It doesn't matter what has gone before all that matters is now. I am compelled to say something that someone wanted to hear more often and I didn't say it then but I do so now always. Everything will be OK.

I recently gave a wonderful little book called Cosmic Ordering to those I loved. I think giving a book is a wonderful gift as it offers so much more, it is adding true value to the receiver, and giving them the freedom of choice whether to read it or believe it or not as the case may be. One of the people I gave it to was my sister in law Jacqueline, who has battled a very aggressive form of breast cancer over the last couple of years.

I was sitting with Jacqueline and my mother when she thanked me for the book and she said as soon as she read it a thought came to her and that thought was that you had to be very careful what you ask for. She then shocked me to the core with her reason for saying that. She said she had been talking with Colin about being a mother, a wife and the busy life that this incurs and in the process had unwittingly and mistakenly wished time for herself, as many of us do, and boy did she get it. Never in her wildest dreams did she think that time for herself would be given in such a way. Jacqueline was thinking about having a massage every week, or maybe taking up a new hobby. The reality was unbelievably shocking, she was diagnosed with cancer.

Well, she told me, *I got a couple of years where it was all about me, but that is not how I would have chosen time for me*. On reflection she realised that although she was busy as a wife and a mother, her experience hammered it home that it was her husband and her boys that were most important to her. Wow! I was blown away by her honesty and self reflection and the power of getting back exactly what you order, so it is vital that you are as specific as you can be about what you want.

The Universe will deliver, but being clear about what we need and want and why is obviously critical and also as stated, it has to be in the NOW. If you state *I am going to try to lose weight*, *I am going to try to be more organised*, *I am going to try this*, all the Universe hears is TRY and it will keep delivering TRY.

Likewise with want, if you continually put out that you *want* something, all it will hear is WANT and deliver WANT.

The secret is simple, we create our own reality. We have the desire and the imagination to do it and our brains make the necessary neural connections when we create the thought and the more we think it the more the neural pathways grow to reinforce it and so it starts to build. We have begun to manifest, to create our own reality.

Talk and think in the present tense, *I am*, *I have*, just as it states in MY Reality sheet. I read this every day and spend as much time as possible creating it both mentally and in turn physically.

My Reality

I am enjoying a fully charged, active, very healthy, vibrant, loving life shared by my family and friends, all of whom I adore and share mutual respect and love.

I am generating a constant flow of income greater than I require as a result of my positive actions, grateful attitude, and by being constantly in tune with the inspiration and intuition gained from my meditation, dreams and joyous awareness.

I am in a nourishing, loving, fulfilling, passionate and mutually beneficial relationship with the ideal intelligent gorgeous sexy women for me.

I have a fantastic home which can accommodate all those that wish to stay with me in absolute luxury.

I obtain a great deal from being able to not only travel the world when I want in comfort and enjoy the wonders that it has to offer but make that possible for my family and loved ones to do so also, and to share in the experience.

I am lucky enough to have a holiday home to relax and enjoy nature to the full and I have all the boys toys a man could want.

I am truly blessed and incredibly happy and wish to share this feeling with everyone that I meet.

My love and gratitude to one and all

David Innes Ritchie

You will note the simplicity and clarity of it all. Most people will have a similar theme but it's important that you create your own by going through a self examination of what you need and want and why and how it will actually improve your life. You then start to look at each aspect individually and make it real by acting on it step by step, heading in the direction you have chosen.

Remember to be careful about those thoughts and the depth and feeling behind them and keep in mind at all times that you create your own reality. You are choosing it every second of every day with those thoughts.

You may be tempted to lash out at this if you feel that you have been dealt a bad hand of cards. It's up to you if you continue to let this fester and ruin your life or you can choose to play a bad hand well. Forget it, let it go, believe that there is only NOW, the past has gone, let it go. The future will be now when it arrives so just live in the NOW.

It all starts with you saying "I am"

In the opening chapter we spoke about water as being the most receptive of the main elements and the mere act of speaking to water can change its molecular structure. We are 90% water, we are thought machines, and our bodies are designed as transmitters and receivers perfectly in tune with the Universe and processing billions of pieces of information per second. Recognise the significance of this, the power of this, the endless possibilities that it offers.

Start playing the game the way it was intended, enjoy it to the full, create a fully vibrant, healthy, fulfilled, loving, sharing life, and have fun playing the game. It all starts with you saying *I am*.

I use this mantra constantly every time I feel myself start to doubt or get angry at people. I still have my traits, like outbursts when I drive and someone does something stupid, and that's because I have 47 years of neural pathways to undo and build new ones.

So rather than dwell on the anger or disappointment, as soon as it happens I accept it, acknowledge it, but then by simply saying

I am in the context required, I start to diminish the old neural pathway and build the new one. I push out the positive message *I am happy, I am wealthy, I am rich, I am healthy, I have a loving partner*, and so on.

Thoughts in action

It is your state of mind that will ultimately have the most influence and is obviously more within your direct control. Does your body function independently of you or do you control your body? Yes the robot in us takes charge of certain functions that would otherwise distract us from doing what we actually do best which is to imagine and to create. We don't consciously tell ourselves to breathe, or our hearts to beat, or our stomachs to digest, but we are in control of it. Let's look at some examples.

Sex is a great one as it's a wonderful attention grabber and we can all relate to it. A man or woman just needs to imagine a sexual fantasy and all sorts of changes take place in the body, heart beats faster, pupils dilate and the most noticeable sign in the man anyway, is he gets an erection, an outward physical sign that it has all worked. Nothing actually happened, it was just a thought created by desire and shaped by imagination.

Likewise by controlling ones breathing and breathing from the abdomen rather than the chest you can eliminate stress and reduce blood pressure. In meditation you can not only tune in more accurately to the Universe, but still the mind, clear the clutter, and focus. All this can be done by one thing and one thing only, and that is thought, yes, just thought.

As usual the evidence is all around us, if we only open our eyes like the Native American Indians, and see it. I am reminded of the saying there are none so blind as those that will not see. Do you understand that statement and the implications?

The power of thought

Let's take it to another level. Let's expand your mind to the possibilities of what we are talking about, let's do some real magic if the above isn't enough for you.

Someone with a nut allergy can just touch a nut to their lips and bang, everything swells up, breathing is effected, a huge physical change to the body in seconds. Was something added? Not really! Yes, one or more sensors picked up the essence of the nut and overreacted but all the actions were triggered by the robot, in this case the robots programme is out of sync or it's necessary because of the persons genetic makeup to cause a severe reaction to protect them, but it was just thoughts in action.

So equally you can effect and change the shape and make up of your body and its state of health, you just need to believe and know you can. Martial artists do this, yogis, mystics etc, you will all have witnessed the mind over matter demonstrations and no doubt thought that they had some special powers that you did not have. No! They just practiced and were disciplined and they believed and they most likely had very good coaches.

You will all have heard of cases where people with terminal cancer have miraculously healed themselves, or a healer has done it for them, not necessarily even in the same country as the person. Or, you might have heard about the women who have summoned super human strength to lift a car or a rock off a child etc. These types of stories are well documented.

Remember we are all interconnected and you can always ask the Universe to help and it will. I did the other day. Someone I care for a great deal had not been in touch for a few months and I was worried about them and I asked in my meditation if they would get in touch if they so wished. Within the hour no less I had an email with an explanation from them as to why they had been out of touch for a while.

For some reason we accept it is possible on the healing level but struggle to accept that we can also use the same gift to improve things not just to heal things. That is partly because of the rules surrounding the creative versus the competitive i.e. if you wish to do it because you wish to be better than someone else then that is competitive but if it's to help you become all that you can be and in turn for your loved ones benefit, then that's a different scenario. So once again we must know what we need, why we need or want it and how it is going to create something better.

For this to work and for you to become TRULY RICH, it has to be a consistent thing, not a gloss or emulsion painted positive thought over a wall of negative thoughts. You need to rewire your state of mind. Some will make the switch in an instant, others will take baby steps. It's all possible, but do it in your own time, there is no rush. Do it properly and you will overtake all those that leap, like the hare and the tortoise. Clear the clutter and rebuild.

Think the right thoughts

A medium was asking a spirit guide what the differences were that she noticed now that she was in the astral or spirit world and she said how everyone in the earthly plane were in such a hurry but were actually in the main going nowhere, and that it was noticeably getting worse rather than better.

Yes, the Universe will deliver exactly what you ask for NOW. You have free will, the freedom of choice, and as such you do not need to do anything that I mention in the exercises, you do not need to think happy thoughts, clear the clutter or anything else for that matter if you don't wish to go for it.

You may well find yourself with the women, the men, the cars, the bank account, and all you want, but and it's a big BUT, will you be happy? Have you wished for something that will in fact make the situation worse for you?

If so, don't worry, it is never ever too late to sort it out. It's all your choice and the game is geared up for it. All I am saying is, just like in construction, would it not be better to think twice and build once, to clear your feet, clear the clutter so that you don't have an accident and ask for the wrong thing?

Life and Abundance and Success

I can feel and sense your impatience, and it is human nature to need to experience it yourself first rather than learn from my experiences so just try it. Take your baby steps or go right in there with all your wants at once knowing they will be delivered. However there is no rush and I am sure you have had your fill of getting it wrong, in going against the flow.

Do your own My Reality Sheet. Write down your desires then start to break them down into smaller and smaller segments. What does your dream house look like? How many rooms does it have? What's in the rooms, and why?

Why will it make your life better? Picture it, feel it, ask yourself if it will truly improve your life? Likewise, do the same with whatever is your heart's desire.

The more you do, the more accurate your delivery will be. However a word of caution, and no doubt this will come as a complete surprise to you and that is that you have to have fun and live life to the fullest at the same time.

Be open and grateful

To become Truly Rich you cannot just think, you must also act, you must give and you must receive, and be grateful for all that you have. Too many of us struggle with truly being grateful when we receive a kind gesture or gift or help from someone else, particularly if it involves money.

We may once again say the words, but our feelings may differ. We may not look at the impact the kind or helpful gesture had on our lives but instead focus on what the gesture meant to someone else. For example you may say thanks, but think it was nothing to him or her, because they are loaded.

What matters is how it affects you, how it helps you. They may well be loaded and congratulations to them if they are, especially if they are happy, but equally they may just appear to be loaded, so all that matters is what impacts you. Their karma will be dealt with separately; you can only deal with you, and likewise if the person can only give you a fraction of what you need but it's all they have, be equally grateful as that is a huge gesture for them.

The key is being open and grateful, genuinely grateful for all that you receive. Don't cancel out your positive message with negative feelings and thoughts. The act of saying grace before dinner and to genuinely understand why you are doing it and to mean it when you do it is just one way.

Another is to always be aware and to communicate that positive feeling and gratefulness into all that you do. Most of all you must be consistent with your message, yes reading your own "My Reality Sheet" will be a good reminder in the morning, but better to memorise it, stick it where you can see it, and every time you catch yourself doubting or going into that negative space, say *I am* and replace it with your new way.

You may say *I have heard all this before, positive thinking and all that*, yes you may have, and they were right, but did you know then why it works? You do now and there is power in just knowing as this opens your inner eye and allows you to see what was always there.

Let me help you some more and show why most previous wish lists fail and why the consistency is never maintained. It comes back to our old friends, fear and responsibility. A great analogy is that of the bull that I have mentioned before but let me elaborate on it further.

Shape your thoughts

When being chased by a bull you have many routes and directions that you can choose to get away from the bull, the only one that you know for certain is wrong is the one going back towards the bull. However, whatever route you take based on fear is full of doubt. *Is this right route? Should I have taken another route? Is there a better way?* I am sure you all recognise this.

Also as soon as you get far enough away from the bull you stop as you didn't choose that route because you wanted to go somewhere, you chose it because you wanted to get away from the bull, from your fear.

Likewise with giving up smoking, losing weight, or any fear based decision. However if your decision is based on a knowing, a loving, a desire, then you only have one choice and that is towards that goal and everything becomes easier as you just ask yourself, *is this taking me closer to my destination or away from my destination? Is it fear based or loving based?*

So taking a common desire such as *I want to lose weight*, why would you ever wish to lose something? It goes against the laws, the rules of the Universe, of creation. What you want is to create the body of your dreams and that's very different indeed, and you can help with your thoughts by shaping it in your imagination and telling yourself I am already that shape.

Help the magic, cut out a picture of the shape you desire, focus on it, remind yourself that you're not going to be, or trying to be, you already are that shape. You are not going to go to the gym, you go to the gym. You are not on a diet, you are not cutting anything out, that's loss again, you are eating things that help create the shape you desire and that's it.

You will be amazed how easy and stress free it all becomes just by knowing what you want, being creative and heading in the right direction with every thought and choice you make. Even wrong choices will become clearer as you know you made that choice and that there is no one to blame but you and you accept the karma.

This applies to every aspect of your life, every aspect. It starts with healthy positive thoughts, keep them consistent, build those neural path ways, and do it, you will be astounded, I promise you, by the dramatic changes, the true magic of the Universe.

Act now, as Good really does come to those that make the effort to help themselves.

Now is literally all you have

Relationships

"All relationships can be likened to a dance and we all learn to dance with each other in a certain way, it does not matter who the relationship is with"

Everything we do in our lives involves relationships, absolutely everything, and therefore it is of critical importance to understand how we interact and react within a relationship.

We have a relationship with ourselves, we all communicate with the "I", our self, our higher self, the person you catch yourself talking to in your head, the person that you call a bloody idiot when you do something foolish or the person of whom you ask, *am I doing the right thing?*

You have a relationship with loved ones in the form of lovers, friends, family etc. and we have work relationships, casual relationships, and relationships with complete strangers, with spirit guides, and ultimately we have a relationship with the Universe and God or Good.

The common denominator in all this is YOU, and this comes back to the key aspect, which is that you create your own reality, especially with your relationships. It begins with a desire, is shaped by your imagination, and manifested by focused action, and so all your thoughts and intentions are played back to you in your relationships. So what makes you who you are?

Well there are a number of contributing factors that combine. You have your spiritual path, the journey that you chose to take in this reincarnation, most will not remember what this is but will feel it, that gut feeling when you intuitively or instinctively know that something is right.

You will also be receiving guidance from your spirit guides either through dreams or those impromptu thoughts that pop into your head, like turn right, or go and get a paper this morning rather than going straight to work and later you realise that by turning right or getting that paper resulted in you getting what you wanted.

Guidance

For those of you who wish to have a better understanding of what your purpose in life is, and in turn ensure that you are heading in the right direction and going with the flow, you have your meditation exercises that will help you become more in tune with the messages from the Universe, your dreams and your subconscious.

You can take this a stage further if you wish and consciously make contact with your spirit guide either through meditation or by asking for it in your dreams or by invoking astral travel (out of body projection) and going to see for yourself, there's nothing better than direct experience.

You can also obtain guidance from astrology, the ancient science that will show you likelihoods, it will also highlight your chosen path and provide guidance to what you need to look at.

I have as I have said, looked at this in great detail as I am a fan of astrology and find it a useful tool to learn more about me and how I can improve my relationships, you can too. However to place this in some sort of perspective, I do not have a chart done daily, more annually, unless there is something particular I wish to look at such as a relationship I struggle to understand.

There are spiritualists, clairvoyants, mediums, and so on, all of who can provide guidance, however, a note of caution. There are good and not so good in everything in life and I would recommend that you trust your instincts and gut feelings and see at least three or four guides to get a better insight into what's right for you. It is also possible to ask the Universe and allow yourself to be guided towards the answer.

We choose it all

So we have spiritual and universal factors that influence who we are in the Universe and the tasks and challenges we require to learn, for example, our own Karmic debt if you like. We also have social and environmental conditioning, and as we have free will too, we can choose to go with the flow or against it.

Remember we chose our parents, we chose our family, we choose our friends, we choose our lovers, we choose our jobs, so whilst you may wish to blame others for how you are or where you are, this is an illusion, you chose it, and you can change it.

I am reminded of the saying *two men behind prison bars and one saw mud whilst the other saw stars.* Both were in the exact same circumstances but chose to react and see things differently.

Two brothers were interviewed and gave the exact same answer to the question *why do you think you are the person you are today?* They both answered, *what do you expect having a drunken abusive father?* One was a hopeless alcoholic, the other a great success.

We can change

So even though you choose your path, you also choose how you decide to look at it. Yes, social and environmental aspects can have an influence but your free will allows you to change that. However we can and should help make this easier for all, especially children, they are like sponges, they are born in tune, aware, and able to do magic.

Some may even be able to see astral beings and auras and so on, and yet we choose to train and diminish all this out of them to turn them into "responsible" adults, which for me is an incredible irony as once again the reality is the exact opposite.

We are training them to be like the other robots or sheep and avoid responsibility. Our children have laser-like truth that cuts through all the bullshit that is virtually impossible to defend. I am reminded of one particular example.

I was driving my children back to their mother's house following my weekend of having them, part of the horrible cycle and fall-out from separation and divorce. My daughter Clare was only four or five at the time and asked me once again to explain why I wasn't with her mum anymore (Cathy, my ex wife). I explained that it was because we argued a lot and felt it better to be apart.

Clare responded by saying *Dad, mum also argues with me*. I said *does she*? She said *yes, and do you know what I do Dad; I just ignore her, why don't you just ignore her too and come home?* I was speechless and couldn't see because of the tears streaming down my face.

In psychological terms we don't have any real sense of self up to the age of three years old. We are happy being a child of the Universe, being at one with all, but by four years old we recognise that we are an individual in this world, we therefore encrypt the programming that will help shape how we react in relationships, which is how the world will see you and how you will see the world, all shaped in that young year. Yes it can be changed but it can take a lifetime or it may never ever happen. In my case it took 42 years.

My personal soul searching

I mentioned that I took time for me following the suicide of my father and the sudden departure of my wife just over a year thereafter, the departure of my wife being the final straw, more like a large tree trunk in reality, and these events stripped me to my core.

All my masks, characters, and coping strategies were forcibly torn away and whilst incredibly painful at the time, I understand my father's actions and never judged him and loved him regardless, and I thanked my wife Shona and loved her no less because what they did allowed me to shine through.

As part of my soul searching at that time I was meeting with an astrologer called Chryss Alexander, a lovely women who also had a highly tuned spiritual element to her and she could see auras. We sort of drifted apart possibly due to the fact that she and Shona were especially close.

I now have an astrologer called Evelyne, an amazing women based in France introduced to me by JJ. Evelyne has become a friend and shares much more than occasional readings with me and has inspired and encouraged me along the way.

Chryss said that the answer lay with my grandmother and that if I wanted to resolve my issue in this life time I should sit with my grandmother before she passes over. I had a slight problem with that as I had lost touch with my grandmother. At the same time as this, JJ had asked me to ask my mother about when I first started showing signs of anxiety.

I did, and apparently it was when my sister started to walk as I was beside myself with worry and always looking out for her, I would have been about 3 years old at the time. So I took it upon myself to ask my mum, who appeared to obviously have a role in my own issues, if I could go with her on one of her daily visits to my Grans.

Chryss had said to me that I wouldn't need to ask my Gran anything directly as she would just tell me the answer and amazingly she did. Out it flowed. It turned out that my Gran married late in life for her time, and she was somewhat reluctant to do so, and shortly thereafter she fell pregnant with my mother.

Her negative feelings about this were consciously or subconsciously passed onto my mother who in turn repeated the cycle with me and as a result, compounded by the fact that I was a difficult baby requiring a lot of attention and stimulus, led to the situation where I learned the only way to feel worthy was through my sister Lynne, who I still affectionately refer to as Pin to this day and who for whatever reason had the connection I sought, hence the reason I was somewhat over protective towards her. Ironically, we rarely communicate now, the pendulum has swung the other way.

This initial behaviour pattern on my part continued until she was a teenager and then I started a process of transferring this issue to each significant female relationship in my life, sadly ensuring that the relationship would fail as a result of this subconscious pedestal I had placed them on and that they could not live up to, and perversely, I would blame them for not doing so. I had to unlearn this.

So that little painful tale that lasted 42 years combines all the factors that I stated at the outset of my chosen path, and it played out in life leading to what is termed a co dependant relationship which is worthy of a few paragraphs in itself.

Changing the steps

All relationships can be likened to a dance and we all learn to dance with each other in a certain way, it does not matter who the relationship is with. Think about it, do you automatically behave in a particular way with certain people? We tend to focus on loved ones when we think of relationships but the reality is we have a relationship with everything and everyone so we have a dance with everything and everyone too.

Keeping it simple, which is the theme of this book, if we wish to change the dynamics of the relationship we need to change the steps in the dance. The good news is you can do this yourself and you do not need the other person's input, because you can change your own steps and this has an impact on the relationship instantly as your dance partner will no longer automatically know your steps and the dance will be changed as a result.

The dance of the wounded souls

Fear once again plays a big role in relationships and I reiterate that if the contents of this book can help eliminate fear or at least get it into perspective then I will have added some value to my existence.

Fear stops people from choosing to change the steps in the dance. One of the most important steps in learning what Love really is, is first to learn to love yourself and to forgive yourself.

My dependence on the significant female in my life began when my sister was born, mainly it would appear because I felt unable to have my emotional needs met by my mother, who in turn didn't have hers met by her mother.

It is worth pointing out that my relationship with my mother improved as a result of discovering all this. I say improved as it was never bad, just misunderstood, in fact the parental roles have reversed somewhat since the passing of my father and my mother regularly and comfortably seeks my council.

My mother is an inspiration to many, including me. She is active, fit, and very attractive and stylish in everything that she does. However, like everyone, only she knows her inner truth and what she is projecting to the world.

It would appear that the reason I transferred my connection to my little sister was because in order to fill my unmet need I tried to fill it by becoming a caregiver to someone who appeared "needy" in some way. This is a recognised symptom of a co dependent individual, which is manifested as an addiction to a person and an addiction to love.

Both parties in the co dependent relationship are afraid of being left or abandoned and they may deal with this differently. Ironically, they become attracted to someone who will *push their buttons*, not a healthy basis for any relationship.

Some will even be perfectly happy to cling on to a dysfunctional relationship hoping that they can change the other person in time rather than change themselves. Others might choose to abandon the relationship not because they want the relationship to end but because they are terrified of being abandoned so will do it first. Unless you learn to love yourself, heal your wounds and stop giving your power away, you run the risk of entering into another "dance of the wounded souls".

Love

What about love? I am inclined to believe that the word *love* is used to describe many things which aren't actually love itself but which imitate something of the properties of love. For example, we can say we love a person, or a flower, or a particular colour or a place, which all have very different meanings. Unfortunately romantic or sexual love for a person seems to be tied up with attachment and insecurity or longing when the object of that love isn't around.

We love our kids but we can accept that they grow up and move away, therefore the same attachment doesn't apply. When we love flowers and colours we can appreciate them in the context that we find them and feel lifted or inspired just by experiencing them. Therefore it would seem that love as a pure form in itself has been grossly contaminated by our social experiences and of course our expectations.

It would seem that from the moment of our birth we spend our entire lives looking for that connection again or for something that makes us feel whole and complete, however, these things can only ever be temporary as birth and passing over are both journeys that we travel alone.

Therefore whatever reminds us along the road of our connectedness or our source, we move towards. Love shouldn't hurt as it is beyond that. It is rejection that hurts.

Rejection can come by physical rejection, replacement with another or even harsh words, anything that separates us out and leaves us isolated. The hurt comes from being reminded that we are indeed alone in a physical sense. That is why spiritual awareness can be so life changing and powerful, it reminds us that we are indeed all connected on a higher plane.

Love as a pure concept in its own right is something that we can only aspire to and we see glimpses of it in many different ways, again, copies of the real thing. We find love mirrored in moments, the rest of the time we feel the love within ourselves and that is what sustains us ultimately. If we don't find the love within ourselves, we cry out in anguish and in pain and this is manifested in anxiety, (separation anxiety), jealousy and all the rest of the things that go with that.

To feel loved is a basic human need and because it is a need, we grab it and try to possess it whereby it immediately slips through our fingers and becomes something else.

Love is something that cannot be possessed, but is passed on and shared. One person can give their love to another but the one they give it to cannot keep it or "own" it, they can only pass it back or on.

I have been in a long-term loving relationship with Irina that I mentioned from Ukraine, sadly, laterally mostly from afar, however we still talk daily and I get a great deal from the wisdom she speaks and the insights from her background and culture. I help her all that I can and we discuss the potential of spending more time together again. I could not have comprehended such a relationship before.

There are many different ways that we can see love mirrored in our lives and therefore there are many different kinds of love, which are all imitations of the concept of pure love itself. Are we afraid of loving and leaving, of commitment and separation? Of course we are, but only because we don't understand the implications and repercussions of fear.

The repercussions of fear

I have stated to my children many times that the only difference between someone labelled a coward and someone labelled brave is how they choose to react, they both feel fear. One chooses to allow the fear to control them, the other chooses positive resistance and doesn't, and once again that is it, it is that simple.

Everyone's fears are on different scales and so it may not always be obvious. For example, two people do a bungee jump, one is terrified of heights and the other isn't and loves the adrenalin rush. The one that is terrified has to summon a huge amount of positive resistance.

In my case, I have learned social skills and appear confident, in fact some say I demand or command attention at social occasions. To the outside world I appeared attractive, successful and intelligent, yet the prospect of going up to a woman that I was attracted to and striking up a conversation terrified me. Don't get me wrong, once introduced I had no issues, but making that first step was huge for me, and my fear of rejection was so powerful that it delayed me, hindered me, prevented me from finding real joy. Even when introduced, whilst I could communicate, I would not share my true feelings if I was attracted to them in case of rejection and would revert to a child like act of pretending I did not care.

Insecurity

Insecurity is one of the most common fears in life today and it can wreck a relationship. I am not sure how much it was felt in the past as this is not a readily documented topic.

I was tempted to assume that given the close knit family units of the past, and the deeply held faiths that communities seemed to have, that insecurity would be less prevalent, however when one considers the fear based religions controlling through reliance on faith and the symbolic worship of artefacts and multiple god figures, and in turn without knowing whether their faith was based on a knowing rather than a longing, we must assume that insecurity has always existed.

I will qualify this as always is a long time and more accurately, I would state that for as long as man has been growing apart from the Universe and the planet that we inhabit.

I suspect that the ancient tribes who lived in harmony did not share this insecurity therefore I refer to the insecurity connected with feeling alone in the world. Are we really alone?

My recent understanding of my own desire to commit suicide was partially that I wanted to return to that place that was safe and all knowing, where I was understood, to the place we call the after world or heaven.

So it could be argued that I have tapped into my memory bank and knew that there was a better place to be and I believe we all have this deep rooted desire to return to that place and that is what makes us feel insecure in this plane as that connection is either not recognized or disconnected due to the way we live now.

Meditation helps regain that connection, as does just knowing about it. One would never miss a cold beer if one had never tasted one. You would never miss a sunset if you had never seen one, and you wouldn't miss a Ferrari if you had never driven one, yet from birth we have one thing in common, the search for happiness. Or put another way, the desire to return to the light.

So there is some logic to support the fact that we remember something we have experienced before and long for it, but as we cannot seem to find it on this plane we feel insecure.

Some believe that on the spiritual plane we are asexual and can reincarnate as any sex, and sex in a form exists in that you can share energies and achieve a high. Once again this makes sense in the desire to bond and have a relationship. We remember the feeling of not only being in the light but also what it feels like to be whole.

There are many poems and songs dedicated to this aspect of feeling incomplete without another. In my own case I note that my desire for sexual gratification diminishes as I become more spiritually aware and I now recognise it as a base or animal instinct. I also recognise that I had confused sex with love and now fully understand and differentiate between having sex and making love.

So when asked are we alone? My answer has to be no. This is coming from one who has felt more alone in this world than most, but has been acknowledged by recognizing the overwhelming evidence of life after death and the intervention of spirit guides in our daily lives.

For example one morning, just over a year ago, in Kiev, Ukraine, I felt like I was going to have a heart attack and pass out and was searching for my connection to gain composure. I found myself talking with my dad and telling him that I may be seeing him sooner than I thought.

Now my security comes from knowing that this is a test bed and life is eternal and that whilst scared as I was that morning of facing death, I had faith to see me through it. So yes I still felt fear but I positively resisted it.

As mentioned above I used to try and find my security in my partner and this was wrong on a number of levels but particularly unfair on my partner as I was placing an expectation on them that they could not ever fulfil as it was my life, so I needed to take responsibility for it.

I used to cringe when I heard people say that you must first learn to love yourself. This was an alien concept to me. Yet others saw me as big headed because they only saw the surface and my attempts to play the game without knowing the rules so I projected the opposite of what I was feeling.

The attraction to sex was based on the release of energy from sex as when you are truly open to it and can lose yourself in the moment you can find yourself closer to the light and what your memory recalls from that realm, however, it can only ever be temporary.

I am so glad that I have now learned the rules and so making love is the icing on the cake, the bonus.

Given the illusion of appearances, and I was a great example, I would also question those that appeared secure in themselves and ask whether it was a faith based thing through knowing, or a denial response not wishing to explore or acknowledge those emotions and feelings? Very few of us are what we appear to be.

Another source of insecurity comes from the fact we are here to experience and learn so if we don't take the time to know why we are here, what our purpose is, then we are confused by the deep down feeling that we don't feel good enough to return to the light and the core as we know instinctively we have not experienced and learned the necessary lessons. That will then project itself into this plane and we find ourselves feeling as though we are not being good enough in life, likewise, we feel we deserve to be rejected.

This is a deep seated fear of being rejected from the light which all combines to make us feel insecure and sadly it is all misplaced, but thankfully easy to change if we choose to do so.

So taking my case, I have suffered terribly from a fear of rejection and as a result tended to ensure I would be rejected as a result of my over protective actions. Now that I am more in touch with the security of existence, I have virtually stopped projecting onto others this keep away from me in an aggressive form to more like hey its safe to be around me thus creating a scenario where rejection is less likely.

Has this created in me an ability to actually go up and speak with someone of the opposite sex? I am heading in the right direction, and the difference now being I add the caveat that as long as it is of the right intent.

At least I understand what is going on now. Part of the lessons on this plane is matching thoughts, actions and words, and being true of intent.

For example, if I am saying I just want to give love and not harm you then ok, if it's I just want sexual gratification without regard for the other person then no, as in my experience sex in this way leaves you empty and unfulfilled and all of us are looking for some kind of fulfilment, to find a sense of purpose and joy in our lives and of course, to feel secure.

What do people truly desire?

To help reinforce all that I say I will show the results from a survey that asked people what they truly desired from life. Not surprisingly, given what we have discussed already, none of the answers were material, tangible or measurable. All were intangible and in my opinion, reinforce my comments above. The top ten answers in no particular order were:

- Personal fulfilment
- Peace of mind
- Relief from fear or anxiety
- Financial security
- Contentment
- Love
- Freedom
- Control
- Wisdom
- Happiness
- Health

So as part of the first baby steps we can take to achieving what we desire we must accept that there is more to life, and that you have your role to play, and that the best thing you can do in any relationship of any kind is first and foremost to stay true to yourself.

Learn to receive

I used to criticise those that I thought were selfish and this was magnified as I sought acceptance through giving, not realising that to be whole encompasses everything. I had to learn how to receive and have only recently grasped this.

My brother Alan very kindly treated my mother and me to a stay in the Monterey Spa Hotel in CA, he did not tell us it was a treat, and he just picked up the tab. I was overwhelmed and broke down; such was my resistance to opening up and receiving. I am rebuilding those neural pathways and opening my heart to all the gestures that people offer me no matter how small or how grand, I am also now fully aware that my other brother Colin would also be there for me wholeheartedly.

So you must also gratefully receive, and if you can be true to yourself, and be just who you are then it's a fantastic solid foundation for all relationships because if someone wants to be with you then you know it's because they are attracted to you, not a character, or an act that will eventually be exposed.

Be true to your path and yourself

Your word, what you represent, who you are, is very precious. Only you can give your word and only you can break it, no one else. Yet how often in even the smallest ways do we abuse this precious gift, like telling someone you had a puncture but really you slept in, or some other seemingly trivial twist of the reality and in doing so you are sending the wrong message out in your relationships and to the Universe as a whole? You are saying that this is acceptable and as such it will be played back to you and just like the chains of habit, the pattern will grow.

So be true to your path and be true to yourself and know that the Universe is a magical wonderful place and that you can create all that you desire, and let this give you, like me, the courage to face your fear.

Yes our worlds will be rocked as that's life, I will feel fear, I will face loss, I will feel hurt and all that's ok and so will you, but it is much easier to deal with if your head is up and you are facing the right direction and you can see it coming.

Feel it, accept it, and then let it go, so that you control it and not the other way around. All easy to say, less so to do, but like everything else the power is in the doing so put it into practice and watch it work.

Is insecurity a form of jealousy?

Now this was another big issue in my life to date and boy what a waste of energy, I have difficulties in even comprehending this now, even though I have felt these same feelings return with those I fall in love with on occasions.

I mentioned in the magic of the universe about thoughts impacting on a cellular level and the building of neural pathways that were addictive. One of the complexities for me, given all that I have said above, and the fact that I was in tune and highly sensitive and had placed my partner on a pedestal, is that if I happen to tune into something that caused me to feel suspicious, I would overreact.

The fear would become overwhelming and I would have a physical reaction that would result in vomiting, convulsions and irrational clinging or rejection, all based on a thought that was allowed to grow unrestricted and as big as my imagination would allow it.

Thankfully I am now able to rationalize and ask myself what I would achieve by being jealous, as she will do what she will do, and in fact is more likely to act negatively in response to my negativity and apparent lack of trust.

Yes it's fear again and insecurity too, and for me it's based on the fact that you think you are achieving the whole and a connection and are scared you are going to lose it, it is going to be taken away from you or someone else will steal it, and worst of all, never regain that connection again.

Interestingly, the never again bit is key because if you believed you would obtain it again, then whilst you would be hurt and grieve you would then look forward to the next connection. Once again, experience teaches you this.

Can we really find true comfort from being in a relationship?

Well we have no choice as everything is about relationships and few of us enter into relationships knowing what we want and expect from the relationship, we tend to react to visual stimulus or neediness.

For example, you think you want a person of a certain type or means or who is wealthy, whereas money is just another way for man to strut his feathers. It comes back to knowing why you are here, where you want to go and why and only then will everything fall into place.

So whilst we all have relationships, the burning question is how do we find that special relationship, a soul mate, that desire to feel whole, to replicate the feeling of returning to the light and combining the yin and the yang?

I accept that in this complex world that we now live, every relationship requires effort and would state that without passion what's the point, and if you can find someone that you can truly bond with, that will give all of themselves as you do, then like the poems and songs say, you will have a taste of heaven on earth. However, I equally accept that you will get something from every relationship.

Wow! Wouldn't it be great to enjoy that connection, that feeling of being whole and secure in this plane rather than waiting for the next plane? Positive, fulfilling relationships are worth it, in fact a must and part of the purpose of life. It is pointless in my opinion to hide away, life is about experiencing, go out and do it, set that watch to tick backwards, don't waste life.

Get out there and live

On that subject, I recently met a fascinating man in the Gym at Menlo Park in CA USA. He was 75 years old and looked in his late 50s. He had recently achieved a target of bench pressing his own weight and set a target this year of marrying his forty something year old girlfriend.

Morten has a list of friends that reads like a who's who and they include 6 Nobel Prize winners. He has written and published 9 books and one movie and advised some of the world's best known companies, yet he was humble to the extreme. He had never owned a television and when I asked why, he said that he didn't have the time as he was too busy living life. So get out there and live your life too.

Nothing happens by chance

In conclusion, when I was going through my soul searching period following the loss of my father and the departure of my wife Shona, I was given the book the Celestine Prophecies to read. I was initially adverse to this as it was a work of fiction and I had a thing about it having to be real and non-fiction.

I now realise that everything is real as thoughts are things, desire drives them, imagination shapes them and focused positive action delivers them.

How do we truly differentiate a physical activity from a dream and say a movie and how many times have you returned from a vacation and it felt like it was just a dream?

This is very significant and to be honest it has just hit me, like one of those eureka moments, as I write this, and that is why it is so so important to just live in the NOW as NOW is literally all you have. There is nothing else as it's either a future event that may not happen or a past event that is already dream-like and can be rewritten so LIVE and ACT NOW.

Back to the point, I read this book and loved it. It carries the message, as I have done in this book that nothing happens by chance, it all happens for a reason. If someone catches your eye you should talk with them as they have a message for you. If you feel that your gut instinct is telling you to go somewhere or do something then you should listen.

I have missed a lot of messages by not having the courage to talk with others, mainly girls that have caught my eye, or I have scared off guys with my glower, or as my children put it Dad is growling again.

Having just read the book I decided to put it into practice and was afforded an opportunity that evening when I spoke with a family who were visiting my local bar. I allowed them to stay at my house that night as they could not get a hotel room in the area and through the passing of time, helped the woman in particular to fight alcohol dependency and go on to build a more fulfilling life.

When you come across particularly difficult situations, learn from them, and find a way through, think positive, there is no better way than this to learn, by looking at the situation and embracing your experiences.

It is only through conflict and change that we learn

The Dai Lama was once asked if he hated the Chinese for invading his country and effectively evicting him, he answered no, it is only through conflict and change that we learn, and we should acknowledge and accept this. He said if the Chinese had not invaded he would not have experienced the wider world and all its cultures and peoples. He was also asked how he felt about people who lied to him and he said he would apologise to the person for making them feel that they needed to lie to him.

We rarely accept that level of responsibility, and instead we prefer to project outwardly, to blame others, and as stated earlier, I was a master at projection. Once again a simple mind shift can change everything, change the steps in the dance.

Accept that your own weaknesses which you project will be played back to you and you can if you wish ask yourself why? Why is this person conflicted with me? What can I learn from this? Why am I making this person so insecure that they feel compelled to lie to me or avoid me? However, don't get fixated on it, just be true to yourself.

It's also incredibly sad that many people are afraid of love and prefer instead to wallow in their comfort zone or create dramas to fulfil and justify their fears.

Whilst we can learn more from conflict this does not mean we should ignore those that live in harmony with us, we should also be very grateful for this too. It's a sad fact that we tend to look at what we don't have rather than what we do have.

I have been married twice and I have mentioned my second wife Shona on a couple of occasions. My first wife Cathy requires a special mention as we have now had a relationship for 30 years as I met her when I was 17.

Cathy has been my wife, the mother to my children Clare and Scott (did a fantastic job), my business partner and still is today, and is without doubt a very close friend. Some people have struggled to comprehend the closeness of our relationship, which is quite sad. Why shouldn't we remain close? Cathy and I have seen and done a lot together and she will always be a very valuable person in my life. It doesn't mean we don't argue of course, there is nothing wrong with arguments in a relationship, in fact it is a positive thing that shows passion, it shows you care, if you did not care you would be indifferent, and conflict brings change. The caveat being, providing the argument is resolved and not repeated.

One of the reasons that Cathy and I have stood the test of time, apart from living in different houses and different countries (just thought I would fling in a married joke), is that we learned to resolve our arguments in a positive fashion. We did not have those skills when we first married but have since learned them and it is something I now use to improve all my relationships.

Dreams have also shaped a great deal of my life and have impacted on my relationships as a result. There is one dream that I wish to share that is about a very personal and close relationship and that is my relationship with an aspect of me.

I mentioned that I used to be an intense angry person, well one night, as I was going through my grieving period and was emerging from my chrysalis or out of the wilderness of despair, I dreamt of a Gorilla.

I can see it still in my minds eye. We were both crying as we were parting company, I said goodbye to it and thanked it for all it had done for me and told it to go and enjoy itself and play with its family and that whilst I hoped I never needed to call on him again that I knew he was there if I needed him.

So I consciously and sub consciously recognised that I did not require an aspect of me any longer, an aspect that was initially brought about or created to protect the frightened little boy who was me but he became over protective and I allowed it to happen until I was ready to take responsibility for myself and face my own fears.

Did I change? To some it may appear that way, but the way I like to put it is that the real me just shone through and came out of hiding.

You see the world based on how you are

On the subject of change there is a very common trait in relationships regarding change and that is once you are with the person you are attracted to, you will often try to change them, which is a contradiction in terms.

The reason for this is that you were not being honest or true to yourself from the outset and having relaxed a bit because you have achieved your desire, you wish to change them to be the person more like who you really are.

Likewise they could be doing the same with you hence the reason so many relationships are embroiled in conflict. Therefore the more you are in touch with you, the more you understand yourself, the more likely it is that you will be attracted to and attract to you the person you do not want to change. Instead you will draw into your life the person you are happy to watch blossom into whom they are meant to be and you find yourself wanting to assist them rather than fight with them, you are no longer insecure or jealous.

I recognise that my jealousy was more to do with my thoughts of being unfaithful than the reality of them being unfaithful. I projected my fears onto them and in turn by persisting with this I gave this energy and was more likely to create what I feared.

This is true of all things, you see the world based on how you are as that is your reality and if you don't trust people it's because you are untrustworthy or harbour untrustworthy thoughts. Think about it, that's what this book is all about, to make you think, make you come up with your own answers.

Learn the lessons

We also cannot discount that the fact that some people are just meant to meet. It is destined, as there is no chance, no accident, and it's up to us to realise that and accept responsibility, to get the best from it, look for the positives, as ourselves what we need to learn?

I have had one such scenario recently where I could not fathom the depth of my feelings for a certain woman, or why I was behaving in such a way, and this compelled me to get a joint astrology carried out, which the woman thankfully agreed to despite her initial negative feelings towards it.

All the answers were there, however before you start getting the new hat for the wedding, there were lessons to be learned from it. I did not pay the astrology the respect it should have had and scan read it, pulling out the validation I sought. If I had read it properly I would have later avoided some rocks that I hit head on and would

Relationships

have been aware of how sensitive she was despite her show of otherwise.

We all have freewill to do what we feel is right, whether that be to go with the flow or against it. Some people need to learn that they create their own nightmares. Everything in life becomes so much harder when we are not true, open and honest with ourselves, when we don't take responsibility for what we think, say and do, and when we point the finger of blame at someone or something else.

I love the exercise about judging people as it is so effective and simple. Judging is to point the finger at someone. Do it now! Point your finger at something and you will instantly see karma and the three times law in action.

Take your focus away from your pointed finger and you will see that you have three fingers pointing back at you. None of us have the right to judge as we rarely know all the facts and rarely take the time to seek them out. The only person we can take and accept responsibility for is ourselves.

Learning and experience are themes running through this book and this equally applies to relationships as we can see, if our bodies did not age, one of the main differentiators between people would be their level of experience. The law of attraction also applies. You will attract into your life those that vibrate at a similar rate to you. Age, colour and creed have nothing to do with it and there will be a reason and a lesson to be learned from everyone who comes into your life.

Write down what you want from any relationship and act NOW like it has happened and you will attract and draw into your life exactly that. Equally if you think life is a nightmare or crazy then that's exactly what life will be for you.

This brings someone I love and care for very much into mind, Fay. Her favourite words were it's a nightmare, or crazy days, she spoke great wisdom at times and touched me very deeply to the extent that I would cry just at her actions of love, which she did instinctively, and yet thought she was doing nothing. It was everything to me.

Ask your friends and loved ones (if you are brave enough) to describe you, it may surprise you but it will be a great help to fast track you to becoming the real you, and in turn attract the right people into your life. We all have the ability to choose. What do you really want? Think about it.

Before concluding I would like to say a big thank you to everyone that I have had relationships with, you all made me who I am today. Also those that lasted the course are truly special and exist because we have mutual respect for each other. Whatever you think I bring to you, you equally give back to me. Those relationships that have stalled or petered out, the door is always open and you will be welcomed back and embraced. I'd also like to say a big hello to all the relationships that have still to come my way.

Finally, I would like to share something I wrote some years past. At the time I was coming out of my grieving following the passing of my father and the departure of my wife Shona. The passing of time and different circumstances has not caused me to change a word and it therefore will no doubt remain a timeless truth, for me anyway.

Accept that you love someone and be happy in that alone. Rejoice in the moments that you can share together

Allow them the freedom to be who they want to be and just be there unquestioningly when they need your support and love.

Give them choices and options and let them decide rather than exerting your will. Your will is personal to you and that strength should be kept for those difficult moments that you need to be true to yourself.

Look closely at those that you feel repelled by, they are equally as special as those that attract you, possible more so in that you will learn more clearly from what it is that repels you than you will from the attraction, which by its very nature will cloud your judgment.

Send light and love and embrace those that you feel negative about, that slight change in energy alone could send them onto a more positive path and you will be repaid three times fold.

Embrace your painful moments with as much vigour as your moments of happiness, both tell you that you are alive and both contain messages for growth, and both shall pass and return again. By embracing them fully you will be able to let them go, freeing up space for the next experience.

Treat all as equal, we are all in search of happiness, but thank those who have brought conflict into your life as they will have either brought to your attention an inward issue with yourself or will have taught you a lesson in growth by the very nature of the conflict itself.

Do not waste energy in questioning others motivation, just be true to yourself and decide wither they fit into your chosen path or not. If not, wish them well and always part company in good faith, you never know when your paths may cross again.

Be clear of thought and true of your intention, as the Universe does not question or make allowances, it merely magnifies and delivers three times fold.

Keep your word as only you can break it and as such it is a very precious commodity.

Accept that anger stems from someone breaking your rules and also accept that they may not know what your rules are, unless you have shared that with them. In accepting this it should dissipate your anger. Anger is a pointless negative energy and a sign of failure and frustration and only breeds more anger.

Protect those you love with your life but never attack unless under attack, even then only use sufficient energy to neutralise the situation.

Embrace the moments of quiet reflection; they are just as important as those moments of ecstatic joy. Be loving and compassionate and live rather than just exist, otherwise you are wasting a life.

Competition versus Creativity

Work and Business

"The Universe is geared up for creation not competition. Competition is a man made thing to make one feel better or superior and to feed the insecurities."

Some may find a section on work and business within a book such as this unusual or out of place, however those of you who have taken the time to read the whole book will have guessed the relevance given my use of business references and business related stories to make a point.

The reality is that business has been a significant part of my life and has helped shape me. Also work and business whether you like it or not, whether it is right or wrong, permeates every aspect of our lives, so all in all its worthy of note and warrants a chapter in the book.

My particular slant has been that of an employer rather than from that of an employee but it's all relevant just the same. Business is a process, and is obviously a man-made scenario, this is worthy of highlighting as business has grown to such a proportion it has almost become its own religion, and sadly a lot of people believe it is actually why they exist.

I empathise with this as I used to be one of them. However in reality it is a means to an end, a way of sustaining ourselves in the world we have created, and the more we create in that form, the more we become dependant on it. In the main business is all about people.

There are process driven businesses, which are less people orientated, but most are relationship based, so if we apply the lessons and rules from this book it will be so much easier and better for all of us all to play the game in the world of business, whether you are an employer, employee or self employed. There is no doubt in my mind whatsoever that the world of business is one arena where one can easily create their own reality.

Interestingly, there is a common thread between lack of academic success and business success. Look at the most successful privately owned businesses, they tend to be owned or operated by people with little or no academic qualifications.

I for one was a frustrated academic who believed that the only way my skills would be recognised and acknowledged would be for me to take the reigns myself and start a business. This was due to the way the current education system is structured in the west, it is for a start, antiquated i.e. some 300 years old, and was originally designed as much to control as it was to educate. It is also designed to be robotic rather than creative and imaginative.

Please forgive any slight on those in the education systems, I am not having a dig at you and the sterling passionate job you do, but at the system and machine that you have to operate within, which makes your task so much more difficult and wastes your energy. The education system does not teach life skills and is mostly irrelevant and is competitive rather than creative.

My brother Colin is a very studious person by nature, but he is also highly intelligent. My family has been blessed in that way, however we are all very different in our approach. Colin did very well academically. He learned early on that if he did every example of previous exam papers he could get his hands on and memorised them, he would sail through the exams, as the content in the exams was largely repeated.

I tended not to study, and had a mixture of arrogance and rebelliousness and a belief that if you learned how to do it then you could do almost anything in time. I did not fair very well in the education system through frustration and other things, and my later exam results did not reflect the esteem or expectations given to me by my peers or teachers in class time.

I am also surprised that we expect our children, or young adults, to excel and to know what they wish to do in life (most adults are hardly great examples) plus we test and gauge them when they are going through a dramatic physical change such as puberty, or is that part of the grand plan?

The main thrust of my point is that the system is once again fear based and competitive and therefore does not get the best out of everyone. Those who struggle academically but also wish to shine are faced with restricted choices of sport, business or crime, or to be humble and return as a mature student to academia.

Likewise however, those who do well in academia struggle to switch to being in business later as they have a fear of giving up what they have and a fear of the unknown.

It is only large businesses that can afford to promote and lobby those who have excelled or are excelling in academia so most in academia are only exposed to large businesses, yet 95% of all those in employment are employed by small businesses.

Large business hierarchies tend to be pyramid shaped, so competition is great. By the time someone realises that they do not fit in large businesses they find it extremely hard to change because of the life style and standards they have created.

My brother Colin did very well in the large corporate environment and was head hunted to join a well funded start up, he is one of the few that took the risk and a few years on he states that unless it was absolutely necessary, he would not return to the corporate world.

However there are also those that did not do well in academia who would excel in the corporate world but have no obvious route for entry as the competition based system requires the certification to allow entry. The result is unhappy people in both camps and therefore businesses as a whole do not perform or create what they should.

Whilst it appears a huge challenge to change this, everything starts with the first step and there is power in just knowing and realising it, in having the ability and opening one's eyes to see what is possible.

What is business?

Like everything in the Universe, the concept of business is actually very simple indeed, from the days of barter and exchange of goods, to the creation of money to represent value. It is the process of taking something, adding value to it and then being paid for that added value, which in theory results in profit. So, the sum of the original plus the cost of the added value is passed on for a sum greater than the cost of the original plus the cost of the added value. That's it really, that's business.

Adding Value

There are a number of ways one can add value. You can make things easier for people, for example by buying something at one location, taking it closer to where it is required and selling it on there. You could make something better by adding something that increases the usability or performance. You can add value by translating or educating, teaching people, making things easier to understand. They all add value, everyone benefits, and on a simple level that's it once again, that's business in its purest form. Add value or a benefit and be rewarded for it.

However business as we now know it has grown in complexity over the many years and not because it needed to, the reality is mostly because of people trying to create mystique and smoke and mirrors about what is happening in order to artificially create added value. Or, to try and demonstrate how clever they are in competition with their peers and justify their positions by over complicating matters, creating the perception of value that doesn't necessarily exist. This is where the problems start as no longer does everybody win as there is no actual added value, just increased complexity and a perception of value.

Marketing, a modern science that grew up around the best way of promoting the added value, has become so adept at the art that it excels in promoting the idea or illusion of value rather than actual value. A great example is a certain type of well known jeans, the original work wear jean that prides itself on not being comfortable and the fact that marketers were able to promote and sell white ones, a contradiction in terms, but a marketing success. There are also many examples where good marketing resulted in a superior product being shelved in favour of an inferior product.

So there are businesses now that are not selling added value but selling the concept of value in the form of exclusivity or designer or leading brands. They may have started by actually giving increased value or better quality, reliability etc. but the bulk of the value eventually becomes perceived value in the form of status.

This led to another business opportunity of ironically stripping away the mystique and guiding people to bargains, designer gear for less cost, and going even further by taking large corporate organisations and stripping them back and increasing the cash value by splitting things up, but none actually add real value.

The ultimate illusion in the business world is the stock market where nothing is created, just the illusion of value that goes up and down, and the brokers make money regardless, and the difference can be sold for cash, another inanimate man made creation that's adds no real value.

We create our own reality in business too

So what's the point to what I am saying here before I move onto my experiences in business and how to apply what we have learned in this book? The point is this. We are not all sitting cross-legged on a beach meditating, and living off the land, we have to acknowledge that this is the world we have created for ourselves.

Can it be changed? Of course it can. Will it change? It has to or we will destroy everything on this planet as the competitive blind race for materialism is what is destroying the biggest asset we have, our home, our planet, mother earth.

Thankfully we are changing it, and necessity is the mother of invention, and we are blessed with infinite possibilities, we just need led or shocked into action.

Am I against business? Absolutely not, the Universe is, as I have stated, a very simple place and operates on simple but uncompromising rules and since we as man are part of this we too are simple, and since we created business, it too is simple. It's simply the act of adding value, and if we are adding value it is a good thing, however lets be clear that adding value is not just adding cash, it's also adding value in the greater scheme of things, improving things for our fellow man and in turn the planet.

The Universe is geared up for creation not competition. Competition is a man made thing to make one feel better or superior and to feed the insecurities. Now the difference can be muddied at times as it can be argued that competition can create creativity and on one level that is true. However keeping it simple, there is no need to complicate matters with competition, we just need to be creative, and if we are creative and add value and you believe in it, you love it, then your business will succeed, there is no way it cannot as it is obeying all the laws of the Universe.

You will create your own reality and people will be attracted to the love and positive energy that you put in. They will benefit from the added value, and you will be rewarded accordingly. You will attract like minded people and so it will grow.

I met a fascinating woman who I was very drawn to at a network business dinner, her name was Tina and she was an occupational psychologist. She specialised in executive coaching and we spent some time together learning from each other.

Part of what I learned from her was the issues surrounding being a charismatic executive, where people are impacted by ones energy. If I was in a good mood then on the whole everyone else's spirits in the company lifted too, and if my spirits were low, so were theirs. Worse still, if I was down they would individually wonder if they had done something wrong and were to blame.

This carried a huge responsibility and once again was a realisation for me that I saw the world differently and others saw me completely differently from how I saw myself. So managing ones energy, ones projections, is as important in the office as it is in life.

We all have something to offer

I once met with Sir Tom Farmer on a one to one business meeting to discuss a potential opportunity that did not come to pass, but we continued to exchange a few emails. Sir Tom is a well known philanthropist and tycoon, if such a word is still applicable. He has been fortunate in his success to have met many of the great and the good in the world, in areas of business, politics, and religion, and can count the Dalai Lama, the Pope and Mother Teresa amongst them.

Keeping the theme of energy going, I naturally assumed that the type of people he met would have had a big impact on him. What he told me both surprised me and warmed my heart. When I asked him out of all the people he had met, who had lit up the room the most, his answer was his sister.

This brings me to the problem with competition versus creativity. In competition, the nature of it means there will be winners and losers, or more accurately, one winner and many losers. So we create an environment where the majority either feel like losers or are chasing an illusion.

One should focus on being the best they can be and not be sucked into the trap of measuring this as competing against someone else. The trouble with benchmarking is that you could unwittingly be lowering your sights or aiming in the wrong direction by comparing or beating someone else. The only target you should set is striving to exceed your personal best and push that limit as far as you can regardless of what others can or cannot do and that applies to all aspects, sadly few will apply this and those that do will shine, truly shine.

Sir Tom Farmer's sister, by the normal scale of measurement and up against all the others, would not be classed by some as a winner but she was clearly not a loser, far from it as we see from Sir

Tom's answer. We all have something to give, something to offer, it may be something as simple as a hug or a stroke of the head.

My friend Fay did not understand why her simple gestures had such a huge impact on me but behind all great people there is a support network and sometimes the people in the background are as great if not greater than the front person. It is therefore much healthier for all to create rather than to compete. WOW! As usual it seems overly simple and all those business gurus will be up in arms about it, but that's it in a nutshell.

Should one be sitting crossed leg on a beach or locked in a retreat? I suppose for a short time they add some value, but real value, real growth is obtained from doing, from experience, from getting amongst people, and as I say business permeates all.

In order to get to your retreat you will have to be engaged with some business or another. Let me expand and tell you some more of my own stories as each story has a message.

My first business

My first business was at the tender age of 14 years old. I attended a local Church Youth Club called the 12-15 club. The disco was terrible and that night I dreamt that not only could I do it better, but I also dreamt how to build it and what it would and should look like. I set about building it, and in another amassing life twist, I was assisted by the lab technician at my school, a Steven Mochry, a grown man in my eyes who unbeknown to me was at the time going steady with a girl called Catherine McFadden who later became my first wife.

Also to add to life's twists, a friend of mine, Miller Robertson who loved to tell everybody we were related (well we were, albeit distantly) won TVs Pop Quiz and Kid Jensons Quiz and became a local celebrity and in turn my DJ. Show me the business plan that could be written in advance and would predict all that. I became the richest boy in the local chip shop, getting 40 quid (80 bucks) a week to buy records and to spend, all this in 1974 when I was only 14.

The point is I dreamt it, I believed it and I delivered it, I never doubted I could do it despite my youth, I only gave it up as I was being sponsored by Wimpey to do a degree in Civil Engineering and this was conditional on me giving up the disco. Ironically I did not go with Wimpey but that's another story.

However I never gave up my desire to be in business, in fact I wanted to work for my Uncle Bill who I worshiped as he was a real character and seemed to have all the good things in life. He encouraged me to get educated and get a job first. I chose Civil Engineering for three reasons.

Firstly, it appeared similar to what my Uncle Bill did but he was actually in building construction, worlds apart in real terms. Secondly, I was attracted to the grandeur of the projects as everything I saw looked big, exciting and challenging, things like bridges, dams, and tunnels. Lastly, because my career advisor in the ten minutes that I met her said it paid good money. I suppose one out of three isn't bad, the projects were big.

My work career

My work career was short lived. I mentioned in going with the flow about my time with Fairclough, the company I joined instead of Wimpey, as it fast-tracked me getting a motorbike amongst other twists. This is the company where I never said no and learned about the fact that there was no such thing as a big job.

I next worked for a transport company; this was more by accident than design, ooops no such thing as chance as we have discussed so let me expand. I wanted more money for my increased responsibility and tender years whilst at Fairclough.

I decided that I needed leverage so I applied for the first job I saw in the papers, it paid great money. Unbeknown to me it was rare indeed for a vacancy to be advertised for that particular company. Also unbeknown to me, I was one of 600 other applicants, another rarity in those days. I was offered the job which was ironic given I had no intention of taking it and only wanted to use it as a lever.

The divisional director at Fairclough called me into his office when he heard of my plan and sat beside me and I learned another life lesson that day. He took a piece of paper and put on one side Fairclough and on the other side the name of the company that had offered me the job. He told me that he would not automatically offer me more money as I should take that as an insult as why was I not valued in the first place.

We did the pros and cons and the new company won. I was sad to leave but another adventure awaited and I chose to accept it. I was now going to get invaluable experience on the client side of the fence as Fairclough was a Civil Engineering Contractor.

It was during my time at this new company that I earned the nickname the Incredible DIR. This was partly due to my eccentricity and forthrightness and the fact that the Universe just kept giving me the answers when I was open to it. In those days I always was open to it, I was generally happy and still saw no barriers or boundaries, life was still very magical.

On the eccentricity front, I once again found that I was quickly accepted into meetings and groups above my station for my age and grade. At one such management meeting I noticed the blank expressions on everyone's face whilst the big boss was explaining something, but no one would say anything. I burst into song singing the then Ultravox hit, "Vienna" with the particular line, "THIS MEANS NOTHING TO ME."

Another time was when the ultimate UK boss was visiting a high profile contract in Berwick with the senior team; it was as if the Gods had descended from the heavens in some peoples eyes. I was an arrogant sod, with little or no doubts, and I had been placed in charge temporarily whilst things were being set up.

The arrival of the big boys caught everyone by surprise. They were all bestowing the virtues of a laser warning system that they had installed to warn if the cliff face moved. I was pouring the tea at that moment and given my youth and the fact that not one of the illustrious visitors knew me, I was being ignored when trying to get my point across. I eventually shouted that it was a shit idea as the lasers were red and were therefore stopping movement at the most dangerous place, which seemed very obvious to me.

Having been noticed, it was then established that I was required on the contract for my skills and I was promoted on a temporary basis to a senior grade for the period of that contract only. For me that was the final catalyst to set up my own business. I was 24 years old in an old mans business, the construction industry in the UK, in the peak of a recession 1984.

However before moving on, I had better tell how the Incredible DIR label eventually stuck. We were on another high profile contract in a high tunnel that was collapsing. We had pumped thousands of tons of concrete and grout in to stabilise the tunnel, but in the dark, smoke filled, artificially lit tunnel, the drillers and us were finding it difficult if not impossible to tell from the drill dust if we were going through new grout fill or rock, and had to leave the tunnel each time.

My father worked in a large chemical corporation, and I asked him if he would ask the chemists at the labs if there was anything that reacted with cement and not rock. He came back with phenophaline that turned purple or violet when it hit cement. I returned to the site armed with a gardener spray bottle filled with phenophaline and saved a fortune in time and resources and the Incredible DIR was born.

Another example was when we were issued with high tech equipment such as endoscopes and heat sensitive cameras to seek things out behind the tunnels brick lining. We actually eventually gave up, cut holes in the lining, stuck our heads in with a torch and used a stick with a spoon on it to get samples.

Ritchie Construction Group

I started my first real business at 24 years old whilst still in employment which I left shortly thereafter, once again I had learned a great deal and I was convinced that I could do better myself. A lack of resources and youth did not deter me and in fact as I have said earlier, necessity is the mother of invention, but naivety is also a great ally as I will elaborate upon.

I had a dream to create a company that carried all trades and it did not bother me what I earned as long as I had one pound or a buck more than I needed.

I eventually created the Ritchie Construction Group which had eight companies within it and received the public accolade from Harry Ewing MP, now Lord Ewing, as one of the great success stories of his 15 years in Parliament.

I achieved a number of industry firsts during this period. We built the first timber frame industrial building in the UK, a training school as part of a design and build contract. We created the first marketing brochure in the sector and were awarded contracts over large international players even though we were not the cheapest.

There are many other stories, however like before, the reason it all happened is I believed it could, I visualised it, and I created it. Problems only occurred when this faith wavered and that came about as we grew in size and I was encouraged to listen to the so called professionals, who sowed the seeds of doubt. Up until then I was always creative, adding value, giving something.

This is true whether you are an employee or employer, one should always be adding value, improving, creating, and making things better. Do you get up every day and think, how can I make things better? Most don't, most look at work as a chore and act purely in a grudging robotic fashion.

All the lessons in life apply to business too

If you are not happy then make different choices, do things in a different way. The fact is it's only fear that is holding you back as by now I should have demonstrated that everything is possible by applying the rules I have shared, and what better place than where you spend the majority of your time, your work or business. Given that business is populated and run by people, then all the lessons in life apply to business and vice versa.

Most people when asked what they want from life don't know as we have discussed. Likewise with business, most owners don't know what they want or what size or shape their business is, or even what their market is. How do they know then that they are going in the right direction? How do they know whether they are running from the bull or towards it? And, if they don't know, how are their employees meant to know? And if the employees don't know, then how do the customers know? And so on.

Before concluding with my overview of what it's like to be in business, I will reinforce another key point, and that is that everything comes to those that are light of spirit, that are happy and grateful, that share. Do all that you can to the best of your ability in the working day, add value, enhance people's lives but do no more than your working day.

It's just like sculpting your body, the exercise is important but equally so is the rest, likewise with work. Live a full life, have interests, have fun, and spend time with your loved ones, that's what creates real success, real wealth, real riches, and real happiness. By doing the best you can in your current role it will provide you with the means to do what you truly want.

Focused effort like focussed light will cut through everything and you will be able to do all you need to do in that focused working day.

I am criticised by some for my apparently leisurely life style. I ask you who has got it right. I am happy, wealthy, and healthy, and in great shape doing what I want and making others happy at the same time. Do I wish to be stressed, argumentative, tired, bad company and miss my loved ones? NO! You choose which you think is the right way.

Is it magic? Well a close friend recently called me Merlin and yes it is magic, but this magic is not exclusive, we can all share in it. We just need to choose to do it, have the courage and not hesitate and there is a friend I met recently that this will definitely resonate with.

My night dreams have increased in intensity and along with this the messages within and I am acting on them now. Let me share some of them with you in the hope that it inspires you to follow your dreams.

Snakes and Ladders

Serge, JJ's partner, a Corsican now living in the North of Scotland, asked me when we were discussing the book if I had devised a game to go with the book. He said that it seemed to make sense that there should be one. I listened and said that I was too busy writing to consider that but would after I had finished.

One should listen to all ideas, especially ones that appear out of the blue. I felt slightly dismissive of him at the time and got on with my writing.

I awoke early the next morning and was alive with the idea of the game. I realised that the basis of it already existed in the form of snakes and ladders and it struck me that snakes and ladders must have a spiritual basis. We climb the ladder of selves and slide down the snake, symbolised in Adam and Eve.

Regardless of whether it is a ladder, steps, beam of light, snake, worm or black hole, the symbolism was there. I also knew what the rules of the game would be. There would be dice to move you along the journey and the outcome of the dice of course can be influenced by you and the Universe.

I also realised that this could be played on all modern mediums and be enhanced so that when you reach the end of the journey, the board or screen would light up brightly as you had created light. It could be a basic electronic board game or internet or DVD based. It would be fun and most of all educational to play and cover all the topics of life, for me, the Ultimate Game.

I carried out some online research and my dream and intuition were once again accurate as the game of snakes and ladders originated in India some 200 years BC and was created to teach people about life, the pros and the cons, the right way to lead ones life. I never set about to think about this, I just dreamt the solution.

You can only see what you believe you can see

Starting to write this book reminded me that I should focus more, I had many opportunities and possibilities but how should I choose what to do?

The answer for me became very evident, and that was to listen to my dreams and intuition. One of the biggest of these dreams, which I have labelled my big global initiative, was actually dreamt 7 years ago and not only has it not lost any of its validity with the passing of time, I have actually had the means to realise it placed on my path in diverse and unusual ways, and it was only when I accepted that I should look at and believe in my dreams again, that I saw all the links.

So once again you can only see what you believe you can see. The initiative involves cash enabling the internet, no credit checks, and no accounts, cash in real time. This will allow billions to access and engage with the internet and explode ecommerce and the internet's reach.

Do I intend to run all my business ideas? NO, my job is to visualise, see how they would work, facilitate and inspire others to do a far better job than I could. So no, they will be passed on and shared, as I have colleagues (one in particular) that are in tune and emerging very strongly and we cannot do everything and we recognise this, so we will keep creating and passing things on.

What if you gave 1% more each day?

So let me paint a picture for you that can be applied whether you are an employee or employer. A leading coach was asked how he managed to sustain his consistent position at the top year after year. He said, *I ask my players individually, can you give 1% more each day?* And they say *yes, as they saw this as an achievable task. This represents a 365% improvement on the year.*

So ask yourself, can I contribute 1% more each day? Don't grudge or judge and resist the temptation to say or think he or she is getting all the benefit so I am not doing my best. Always do your best, it will open the doors and give you the means to do what you want to do, just get in the habit of always shining.

I don't do something because it gives me 1 or a million bucks, I do it because it feels right, and I do it to the best of my ability. I should actually qualify that, that's how I started, when I intuitively believed in dreams and infinite possibilities, and that's how I am again now that my faith has returned.

There was a period in the middle where I allowed the doubts and negativity to take hold and got caught up in the competition rather than to create and add value.

So how do we achieve successful status? Well what very much comes to mind is that we MUST all pull together (push is actually more appropriate as I will explain later). The first image that comes to mind is a symbolic one from the animated film Finding Nemo. There is a scene where a school of herring have been caught in the fishermen's net, a huge catch for the fisherman. The herring are in a panic and frantically swim in all directions to try to escape, probably making a bigger effort than they have ever made in their whole life, but sadly to no avail, as whilst the net bulges, the ropes creak and strain and the crane tips, the net is still being lifted out of the water.

Young Nemo encourages all the herring to swim in the one direction and slowly but surely they do and the tables are turned, this same energy focused in the one direction topples the crane and breaks the ropes, mission accomplished.

Also, can you imagine the combined effect of a whole team who each have improved 365% year on year pulling in the one direction? So yes if WE all pull together with a common aim then we will achieve more. Will we succeed? There are no guarantees, yes it's more likely, but the path to success is not linear. In fact there is a widely accepted paper on the five steps to business success and this can equally be applied to life, with each step representing a required change in the business to move to the next level. However whilst any change represents an element of effort and with it pain, it does not adequately paint the picture of what is required.

Getting to the top of the hill

The image that best represents the journey in my mind is a follows. Rather than picturing a flight of steps, picture a series of hills, one higher than the next, with the base of the next hill's sloping accent beginning below the summit of the last.

If any of you have done any hill walking or climbed Munros you will picture exactly what I mean. As soon as you get to the top and heave that sigh of relief, then look up, you realise it's not the top and there is another summit to climb.

Now picture a HUGE coin the size of a house. I use the imagery of the coin deliberately because although not ideal, money permeates our entire society. The task in hand to achieve success is to push that coin right to the top of all those hills and at the top a slot will await for the coin to fall into and as a result a large payout will be made for all the efforts.

Now amongst us there might exist a super human who may be able to push that coin alone to the top of the first hill, but even then in reality they are likely to fall exhausted, unable to go further.

To get the coin up all the hills requires a concerted effort from everyone pushing in the one direction. And like everything that's uphill, it grows harder as you get further up as it's not only steeper but you also grow tired. This is where team effort is essential as when you grow tired, doubt and fear creep in, weakening the belief and as a result some may stop pushing momentarily. We will all feel this as it suddenly becomes noticeably harder.

Now the danger here is twofold. If one or more also stop pushing to either lecture or criticise the person who has faltered, then the coin could roll back and we will all have to start again, with less energy than before, and also with bruised confidence. Or, if we do get to the top we could be so tired with the excess energy that we had to expend with the loss of the others that it will make the next hill all the more difficult. Worse still is not someone simply dropping off, but someone actively pulling others back.

Unfortunately we are not very good at embracing what we have in life, but experts at complaining about what we don't have, and sadly that can spread very quickly and exponentially. So if someone does falter, you must keep pushing, but also at the same time hold out a helping hand, so they are not left behind. This act will bolster their confidence and belief that they are wanted, and will galvanise their effort when it's confirmed they are not alone. However if they start pulling you back, wish them well, but let them go and get back on with the job of pushing.

They may in the future reflect and come back up the hill to lend a hand once again. If so, don't complain about their indecision, just welcome the fact that they have rejoined the team having reflected and are therefore more likely to stay the course having overcome their own mental obstacle. They have chosen to do it rather than just been swept along and so they must be welcomed back in.

Getting to the top of each hill carries its own dangers. The coin will feel lighter with the euphoria of reaching that milestone, it also may appear to gain momentum of its own accord as it rolls down to the start of the next hill. But the laws of physics will apply and without continued support and energy the coin will only roll as far as the energy that is put in and then it will start rolling back.

Now for some, the next hill may seem very daunting, or they are too tired, or they have just reached as high as they want to. There is nothing wrong with that as life is all about choices.

There is a saying in both the worlds of psychology and spiritualism that you should not complain about where you find yourself today as it's a result of the choices you made in the past, and equally you can make different choices and find yourself in a different place tomorrow.

So as above, wish those that wish to stay well as it's their choice and choices can change. Dwindling numbers will quickly be made up with fresh strong people, some possibly even more experienced than us, all wanting to join us in recognition of us reaching that milestone. The coin will also be more visible the higher it goes and therefore attract more people and so this goes on, up and up the hills, with changes at every stage and tests along the way as we grow exponentially.

Now I may have painted a picture that whilst it's not linear, it's only a matter of sustained team effort, support and recognition, that there will be changes and casualties along the way. Wouldn't it be wonderful if life were that simple, like hill climbing? It's not just a case of going up, direction is also important too.

As discussed earlier, when you know where you are going then decisions are easier about whether you are going in the correct direction or not. Is this taking me where I am meant to be going or not and is this filling my cup or not?

So we must know where we are going, yes we are going to the top, but there will be hard routes and easier routes and obstacles in our path. The secret is to use the more experienced to help choose the best routes. The reason I say help rather than show, is the young and naive can equally show us a better path and we should not be blinkered to that fact and should be open to all possibilities. I for one have beaten a path that my elders at the time would not have considered so the secret is to listen to all then do what feels right.

Now this is were we need a clear vision of what we wish to achieve and all share in the same map. Like all maps things change and unexpected obstacles will come our way, this is the real test for success as we must not be despondent, we must accept that it is life and all part of the journey and work together and find a new path.

Our leaders or coaches must have their heads up and eyes open and not just be pushing the coin, otherwise we will miss opportunities and better paths and we should encourage this and be thankful of this and constantly feed them accurate information to assist them with their task.

We should also recognise the times that they lead by example, when they join the push, as both are equally important. We must all take time out to go and have fun, get refreshed, play, and in doing so, we may stumble upon a better route or come up with a new strategy or tactic rather than just robotically pushing and pushing regardless.

I love the analogy in body sculpting that the rest is as important as the effort and once again nature shows us the way.

We will all have different roles in getting the coin to the top. Some people may drop off as we go, and the team members are always free and welcome to join another team therefore providing a safety rope for those who would otherwise be afraid of starting the climb if such a safety rope did not exist.

Ultimately each summit will bring new choices, new routes and new people, but one thing should remain consistent, our mutual desire to get to the top, whatever that entails.

I have in life been very lucky in that I have learned the difference between need and want and how to manage expectations and having examined it all. I WANT to be the best that I can be, and I KNOW I CAN DO SO.

I welcome all those who wish to join me on the journey, the journey of endless possibilities, the ultimate game, the game of life.

Children enter this world still in touch

with the other world.

Inspire our children

The Future Happens Now

"Think about the change in you when you feel the sand between your toes and the blades of grass on your bare feet"

When I started to write this chapter, I initially felt slightly uncomfortable as I had strongly made the point that all that matters is NOW and yet here I had a title called The Future.

I have also stated that it is only on this plane that time has any relevance, so given the fact there is no time, and that evidence is being collated to prove that all we have is NOW, it placed a question mark on the title The Future. However, as has been the case throughout my life, and in particular when writing this book, the answer just pops into my head, so the title changed to the Future Happens Now and I instantly became more relaxed and comfortable.

Writing this book has been for me one of the best things I have ever done. It has been immensely therapeutic and has given me great clarity and certainty, and whilst I have not entirely eliminated fear yet, it has given me the courage and determination to have positive resistance to everything negative in my life, including fear.

I sincerely hope that I have touched something in you also, and if nothing else, stimulated a constructive debate and a continuous search for the answers. I have not claimed to give the answers, just the rules to help you play this amazing game of life, and I have shared my own personal opinion with you.

I would also like to share with you some of the mental games that I play and have always played. It is said that once you expand your thinking, it can never return to its original size. I have been exercising my own thinking, and therefore my brain, all my life, but just like any muscle I may not have always been doing it in the correct fashion. It needs to be fed, to rest and to be nourished, and I have not always looked after it, especially, I have indulged in excesses of alcohol, but nonetheless, I have been exercising it just the same.

As a pubescent teenager fixated with the opposite sex and their bodies, I would imagine how many girls were in my street and what were they up to. How many were in the town, city, district, region, country, nation, continent, world, and this went on until my brain hurt. As I matured and moved away from the tortures that puberty can play on us, I adapted the same pattern with how many species of life there were and how many ants, insects and so on.

Shona, my ex wife and I used to play games with how we could do multiples and arrived at things like beans, lentils, dust to infinity, to show how much we loved each other. If I had known about quanta or quarks at the time I would have added that.

The reason I mention this is that I personally obtain scale and a greater level of understanding when I play numbers games as it helps me to understand and quantify things. This is something that I think we should all do more often in order to get things into perspective and to help us question the paradigms and of course to steal the control away from the robot.

A great example of scale and fear is the shark. Sharks kill approximately 4 to 10 people globally each year and yet due to our lack of scale and perspective, we kill over 26 million sharks every year and many shark species now face extinction. Who should fear who?

I came across another example on television recently. I rarely watch TV but when I do, I generally find something on that relates to my current interests and this may be synchronicity at work or just pure coincidence depending on where your school of thought is.

In other words, is there such a thing as an accident or exceptions to the rules or is everything mapped out for us? I personally believe that everything is mapped out but we can and do wander off that path and these acts or examples of synchronicity are signposts to prompt us to get back on track and we can choose whether to follow them or not.

If we ignore them, they can become bigger and louder and ultimately unavoidable, manifesting in some cases as illness in order to force you to stop and consider what you are doing. It can take many forms and some people may choose to ignore them for their entire lives.

What are we capable of?

Back to the point of scaling and putting things into perspective, the programme was about a father who stimulated by his daughter's very early interest in Chess, pondered and then experimented on whether a genius could be created rather than born. I have to say that whilst they presented an interesting argument which highlighted something else for me, they did seem to gloss over the fact that it was the child who asked the father to teach her and not the other way round. This was a key point for me.

However, the point I wish to make is around scale. The girl, having achieved Grand Master status at the age of 21, a rarity indeed as few females play, and of course she was also very young, was subjected to brain scans by scientists to see what they could find.

They discovered that what she was using was the same part of the brain that we use for face recognition and that she had trained or adapted the process to recognise known chess positions in a similar fashion to how we remember faces. They discovered that it had to be known chess positions as when they scrambled chess pieces, she reacted as we all would to such a scenario, however, when shown a board with pieces laid out as a chess player would have them, she recognised them instantly, in fact, in 0.8 of a second.

To put this in some sort of perspective, there are 4 billion potential chess positions and she was able to access all of them in 0.8 of a second. This may sound staggering until we apply scale and perspective and remember that the brain is apparently processing between 40 and 400 billion pieces of information a second so the instant recognition is well within its capability.

It also demonstrates what we have discussed before about mechanical thinking. If she had to think about it then the pure mechanical thought process would take longer as she would have had to sequentially go through all the possibilities and that could take forever.

So just like a top sportsman or any other highly trained individual, thinking doesn't come into it. A good example would be that of a racing driver. If he had to think about every manoeuvre he made he would undoubtedly crash. At those kinds of speeds it would be much better to have ones vibrations high and allow information to intuitively pop into ones mind and to trust the answer.

We all feel and know the truth so with discipline and practice we can all tap into power sources that may seem nothing short of magical to others. The truly fascinating aspect for me is that I sense we are barely even scratching the surface of our true capabilities.

Scale and perspective

The enormous population explosion on the planet in the last 100 years is staggering and currently shows no immediate signs of easing up. In biblical times, some 2000 years ago, the population numbered 250 million globally, approx the population of modern day America. By the turn of the 1900s we had hit 1 billion and now in 2007 we are up to 6.5 billion.

Even the most basic mathematics could plot the graph and go WOW what has happened? Not only is this an issue for me from a perspective of sustaining the planet, as we now exhaust the earths produce by September of the year i.e. by month 9 , therefore we are in deficit and are therefore already bigger than what the planet is able to currently sustain, but it also raises questions over why so many souls are being sent or requesting to go to the planet now. Had I got my beliefs all wrong? Were the evolutionists correct, even though their evidence trail has huge gaps and modern science and recent discoveries is widening those gaps rather than closing them? Were we just a rapidly growing virus destroying its habitat as all viruses do?

I truly struggled with this for a while until I realised I was measuring things using my limited understanding of time and not in universal terms.

There is no time, it is merely an illusion, and therefore the increase in souls in this dimension could be argued and in turn justified. The ancients that I have touched upon many times throughout this book state that we have been around for a long, long time stretching into many millennia.

Many, many civilisations have come and gone of varying degrees of technology and civilisation much of which we are only guessing at from the clues left behind either in passed down stories or the artifacts that we struggle to explain the discoveries of which are on the increase rather than decrease. No doubt if we ever have the ability to properly explore the ocean beds and below the ice caps we will discover much more. It would seem reasonable to assume that if we struggle to grasp their existence, technologies and cultures we equally could struggle to grasp the numbers that they existed in.

However I accept that this, like much of what we have discussed, is not easy to compute or grasp. So let's also do the numbers game to help put things into some perspective. Each of our bodies contains 10 trillion cells, all containing the ability and DNA to recreate you in your own likeness, we are our own Universes.

To be clear, what I am talking about replicating here is the vehicle, the carbon shell, the robot, not the driver or the observer or the energy being.

Let us also consider our understanding of time for a moment. We once again say the words but do we actually truly grasp the concept? We all readily talk about dinosaurs as if they only recently disappeared yet we are told that they existed 65 million years ago. Can you really compute what that actually means? Plot the graph and try to find a piece of paper that can show in a reasonable scale the span of your life in relation to when the dinosaurs walked the earth.

The oldest living, growing thing on the planet is the giant redwood trees. They live for a few thousand years, a staggering time compared to our 100 years maximum yet even they barely register on 65,000,000 years, so time in that sense is difficult for us to compute.

The years fly by as you get older but hold your breath and it seems like an eternity so there are many confusing aspects to the concept and our understanding of time.

I have also been lucky enough to have been able to travel and whilst I have not visited every country I have at least visited every continent and in all my travels I have never met a single human being that I thought was soul-less. Yes, many were robotic and sheep-like, but it wouldn't or didn't take much to wake up the spirit within each one.

So there must be a reason for this explosion of souls on earth and all I can think is that it is necessary and we will be facing a large event that requires this. Global warming or an asteroid collision or the forecasted tipping of the earth's axis immediately springs to mind but I am merely speculating. Or is there a limited window of opportunity for many to obtain a particular experience?

One thing that helped me get things into perspective, which I will share with you, is that I recently watched the Al Gore film, An Inconvenient Truth, and it was both fascinating and alarming regarding the potential future of our planet.

I have to say that at the tender age of 47 I have watched a number of films in the past and read "end of the world books" all of which were alarming, but do they give us a big enough fright to shock us into action?

What strikes me the most in An Inconvenient Truth is when they showed pictures from spacecraft as they flew from the planet. Initially it was awe inspiring and very beautiful, and eventually it became no more than a pixel on the photograph, which forgive the pun, brought me back to earth. Our planet, large as it is, especially if you start from yourself and expand your mind around the globe, is in fact, only a speck in the Universe.

For some reason I was at the same instant reminded of our own bodies, so if you like I stopped looking outward and started to look inward, and realised that whatever scale I considered outward was reflected inward also. So for example, as stated above, 10 trillion cells make up our body, and the fact that each of these cells contains sufficient memory and DNA to replicate our bodies is mind blowing, and then I was reminded that we are one with everything and this is a key point.

Unnecessary divides

One of the issues we face as modern man is how separated we have become rather than how connected we actually are with each other, with nature, and the Universe as a whole. This feeling of being separated allows fear to take root and grow and fuels the blame culture, looking at what divides rather than what binds us.

The famous Scottish bard Robert Burns stated *oh to have the gift to see ourselves as others see us*. This would without doubt eliminate the arrogance that sadly helps fuel the unnecessary divides between peoples and cultures. We have some terrific examples of this that once again may appear flippant but it highlights a common theme and will also allow more people to relate to it.

For example the World Series, which only contains entrants from the USA. In the West we talk about the best movies in the world but in reality we only talk about Hollywood and ignore Bollywood in India, which in many ways dwarfs Hollywood. Again this may seem trivial but they are examples of how we create division or separation rather than cohesion.

We are all MANKIND and all share the same universe and are connected and we should celebrate this but instead we are guided and cajoled into distancing ourselves from each other and from nature and the universe too. It appears to me to be no accident and the Machiavellian rule of divide and conquer seems to be actively in play throughout history, the question is by who and why do they seek and require control?

What we require is a mind shift, a change of focus

What does all this mean and what do we learn from scaling? What is it all about and why are there so many of us? It can be argued that the vast numbers of people are merely the result of increased access to food through technology and improved medical practices with no spiritual component or universal meaning.

I would counter this by reminding people that the men who created technology or improved sciences in the majority of cases talk of Eureka moments or flashes of insight. Many of them dreamt their solutions out of nowhere. It could equally be argued that they were given this knowledge in order to sustain the growth for a greater purpose.

We cannot see quanta but it exists and reacts, it is thinking stuff that permeates a Universe that we cannot fully grasp. So what are we to do? I believe that either a global event or a great leader will inspire all those souls into positive action. In fact it can happen in an instant, just flick that thought switch in your head now and make others aware and see if they too choose to flick that switch.

There was an experiment conducted in New York where 4,000 people were brought together to meditate. The New York police were part of the experiment to validate it. The active meditation brought down the crime rate in New York by 25% during the period of meditation and the Police commented that only 2ft of snow in summer could have had a similar impact. The fact is, it did, it happened. An interesting thought is perhaps global warming will also give the police their two feet of snow in summer. Which would you prefer, meditation or snow in summer?

If the people of the past could use their combined energy to create magic, i.e. influence their surroundings and achieve things that we struggle to grasp today, then I am sure that 6.5 billion people all following Nemos lead, can impact on the quanta and manifest what is required in our combined chosen path.

So in recognising and accepting we are immortal, I remain an optimist, especially as there are clear signs all over the world that spiritual awareness is on the increase, in books, music and movies, which all reflect this awareness along with the fact that science and spiritual or ancient knowledge are merging and validating each other.

All that remains is for the religions to also openly and actively engage in the debate and in doing so will see that it is not a threat but a reawakening of the original teachings that have been hijacked and politicised in order to control.

Given that we are immortal spirit energy beings does this mean that we do nothing? Absolutely not, it is our responsibility to recognise this and do something about it. We have to face the truth of how great and powerful we really are and take responsibility for it, and as it sates in the song, it all starts with the man in the mirror.

No one is born into this life to be destitute, wretched etc. unless they choose to be, and equally you still have the freewill to choose to change further. There is abundance in the Universe and we all have the ability to share in this abundance.

They say necessity is the mother of invention and global warming and population growth is ensuring that it is necessary to start to follow the laws of the Universe and create, learn and grow. What we require is a mind shift, a change of focus.

This on one level is as simple as throwing a switch in our brains and building new neural pathways, however given the addictive routes that we have already created then there has to be a compelling reason to do this. I say addictive because our thoughts stimulate the release of chemicals that gives us our emotional fix.

Yes we can rationalise we are doing something wrong but we still do it because we need that emotional fix and sadly need to be shocked into action. Let me give an example.

If you placed a frog into boiling water it would immediately jump out, but if you placed it in normal water and started to boil it, it would remain there until it was boiled to death. Sadly, we behave like frogs.

That is why experience or playing the game and actually doing something about it are important. We could be told all day long about the facts but unless you witness it first hand it means very little to you unless you had previously experienced it. Some of us have experienced more than most and therefore can empathise.

The good news is that things can be accelerated by knowing, so rather than blindly experiencing and not grasping the bigger picture, if you know what the bigger picture looks like you can quickly validate your experience and know that you are heading in the right direction. In doing so there will be a critical mass effect that when a certain number on the planet all start to think or believe in the same way it will tip the balance and accelerate the progress.

Look at the reality

Virtually everyone in the world must be aware of the war in Iraq at the moment. However their perspective will be coloured by what they have personally experienced, and what they are being shown and told. People in the USA and UK and associated allies will relate to the soldiers being killed, of whom there have now been over 3000, and people in Iraq and their neighbours will relate to the hundreds of thousands, some say as much as 650,000 people that have been killed.

The fact that the west, in particular the USA news media, promotes the death of the soldiers and glosses over the civilian totals is interesting in that there would appear to be a conscious effort to maintain a level of fear.

We therefore need to look at why things happen and not just what has happened, it seems so simple, but we generally don't do that. In fact scarily, we can get caught up in what might happen as part of the fear mongering forgetting we can actually get things into scale and perspective and choose to act to shape the reality.

This leads me to our preoccupation in life with bad and negative news. There is a bit of a vicious circle going on here and at the root of it is our avoidance of responsibility. We complain about all the negative things in the news but the media owners openly state good news does not sell.

So whilst there is a need to expose wrong doing it should always be kept in perspective, in scale, otherwise the minority start to control the majority through fear. Just like we forget that Santa Clause only wears red because of Coca Cola, we start to believe all politicians are bad, all priests are perverts, the USA are heartless capitalists, Arabs are terrorists and so on whereas in fact the reality is completely different if only we care to look. It's as if your only frame of reference is negative, then eventually you forget the good and only see the bad.

Shedding responsibility leads to fear

So why do we allow the negative to continue? Why does bad news sell and yet good news doesn't? Basically it gets back to our unwillingness to accept responsibility for the fact that we are the creators of our own reality. That is too scary for us so if we see bad things it is a more comfortable frame of reference, *I am not as bad as that, see I am a good person* etc.

We lower ourselves to the lowest denominator rather than strive for the highest. There is also a benefit for some to maintain the perception of fear as a very efficient and effective controlling mechanism.

We claim to put our faith and trust in politicians and religious leaders where in fact what we are doing is attempting to shed responsibility. The laws of cause and effect scare us so let someone else do it and blame them.

Let me bring it back to a simple level and you will either relate to this as the initiator or the victim. Both my brothers, to different degrees, display a negative trait that I used to be an expert at. That is, asking their partners to do something that they themselves either do not want to do, or are fearful of doing. Then they fall out with their partners because they did not do it the way they wanted it done, so they avoid the responsibility and blame someone else. This trait scales up the country to government level.

You may smile and, why not, it's great to smile, however this is at the root of what is stopping us all from playing the game to its fullest. This shedding of responsibility has led to a fear filled world that has lost its scale and perspective and allows the few to control the many.

USA and UK justified invading Iraq due to weapons of Mass Destruction that did not exist, they played on fear. The respective leaders may have believed what they were being told and also reacted out of fear, only they know the answers to that. Other countries react negatively out of fear, seeing what has happened and then think they could be next, especially when the justification appears to be skewed.

Terrorists are ironically given magnified control and importance and as a result, they are able to disrupt travel, commerce and so on, in case they do something else bad. Forgive me for over simplifying things but I truly struggle when I apply scale and perspective to justify or understand why all this is permitted.

I hear the arguments that every life is precious and therefore the killing of one person in a terrorist act justifies a response, or even worse, a pre emptive strike based on what you think is going to happen. Do we value lives from different cultures and countries differently? It would appear that we do and where does all this start and stop? Once again it all comes down to experience. If you had killing on your doorstep you would understand the cause and effect.

We must try and open our eyes and get things back into scale, back into perspective, to be free from fear and enjoy life and our neighbours and our world. Is someone likely to want to kill you if you treat them with love and respect? Do unto others as you would wish done unto you. Fear blinkers and skews our vision and causes us to retreat into our own little comfort zones, our own realities.

A recent analysis looked to see why the USA was so violent internally. The answer that came back was FEAR. The country was fearful and was attacking itself internally out of fear, just like any animal in the jungle it would prefer to avoid violence unless through necessity to eat, as violence risks injury and therefore threatens its future, the only exception is when it lashes out through fear.

We have now extended this avoidance of responsibility and fear filled response to our children, which is both sad and very scary. Children are no longer allowed to play and experience the world as freely as they should in case something happens to them or the school gets sued because they get hurt playing in the playground and so it goes on and on.

Does this protect the child? Far from it, it damages the child for life, it creates fear from the outset that is disproportionate and restricts their development and ensures the perpetuation and growth of the fear myth until eventually everyone has forgotten why. Instead of playing outside they are exposed to the adult's world of negative news and media and so the vicious circle continues and is in fact accelerated.

We have to stop this fear filled reaction, we have to gain perspective again, we have to go out there and play the game, experience life, skin our knees etc., as the reality is we have nothing to fear but fear itself. We have all the answers if we only care to lift up our heads, open our eyes and allow ourselves to see. There are indeed none so blind as those that will not see.

We have all the technology and knowledge readily to hand to make a difference but we choose not to use it

The biggest living organism in our lives is what we used to refer to as mother earth and we used to respect it like we should a mother, but we have become arrogant and lost touch with nature. We watch it on TV and movies and get a sense of it, but this is nothing compared to experiencing it.

Think about the change in you when you feel the sand between your toes and the blades of grass on your bare feet. The clues are all out there, it ironically brings you back in touch with the Universe. We have become human battery hens.

Nature has played this game a long, long time and holds all the answers as there is nothing new in this universe, it's just a manipulation of what already exists yet we still wish to try and compete with her or ignore her rather than learn from her. Ooops forgot there is no profit in that, sorry just being sarcastic.

Ironically there is profit in it, it's a long term investment though, in fact the ultimate long term investment, as the current short term view is destroying our principle asset, our home, our base, so we won't have a business shortly and money will be irrelevant.

We have all the technology and knowledge readily to hand to make a difference but we choose not to use it. There are many arguments levied about why we cannot afford the new technology that will save us and our planet but this again is mostly an illusion and a manipulation by those with a vested interest in maintaining the current, damaging ways.

It belies belief that we value pieces of paper more than our planet and the future of our children and our children's children. We obviously only feign love because if we truly loved our children, our home, our planet, we would not hesitate to take action and certainly would not place money as the main obstacle in our paths.

The ancients seem to have had it right. They respected the earth and their fellow man. They embraced other tribes but recognised their differences and did not try to assimilate them into their cultures like the Borg from Start Trek or in reality, like so called civilised man.

The Native American Indians even tried to help the explorers and shared their food with them, even saving their lives at times, isn't it interesting how they were repaid?

History also shows that all major civilisation expansions were brought crashing down when they could no longer feed or sustain their expansions. The dramatic growth of man has been as a result of embracing and harnessing new technology and adopting mass production of new food cycles. This could have been sustainable yes, but why isn't it?

The simple answer is once again, money. Every new advance could have had a counter balance but the search for profit means that the focus was elsewhere and nothing was put back unless it made a profit and soon, we will have raped and pillaged our ultimate asset to such an extent that it will have to be a natural correction that takes place, most likely in the form of a cull on a monumental scale.

Here is an ironic and shocking example. A great deal of the rain forests are being cut down for agriculture, in particular beef farming, and even more precisely, beef farming for hamburgers i.e. fast food. So we are destroying our mother earth for short term gratification in a burger and a quick buck.

The rain forests and trees in general have been greatly underestimated in true value. One rain forest tree can have as much as 40 acres of surface area if each leaf is measured, so forget the acres of trees, do the maths and scale it up by the number of trees and the actual acreage being lost out of our natural CO2 recycling engine.

Trees, like all plant life have a dramatic effect in the life cycle of air on our planet. They absorb CO2 and produce Oxygen, they create topsoil and adjust water tables and yet we destroy them in their millions daily and replace them with what?

Likewise we talk about the disappearing ice caps and glaciers and the wonders they offer without even looking at the benefits of the cooling effects and reflective advantages they have for our planet.

In each and every case we have the combined ability to make the decision to do something about it and use the new technology that we have created in a positive manner to carry this out. We can save our planet and our fellow man. So why don't we?

Money

Once again, it is our misplaced love of money that prevents us, this simple man made commodity that has assumed the status of a God. Once upon a time it had at least a perceived value as it was tied to gold standard, which in reality was just another commodity that we placed an illusory value upon but even that relationship has been severed leaving the manmade tokens we call money to stand alone.

Doing something about the planet might just have a negative impact on the economy and that just cannot be allowed. Shocking isn't it? Al Gore's film has a wonderfully simple example of choice, a set of scales with gold on one side and the planet on the other. Which would you choose?

I saw another example of the misplaced priority on money when I heard Hilary Clinton rhyme off the benefits for the future of children by attending Kindergarten and she reckoned they had an economic case to justify it. Pardon! When and where did we forget that we created money, it's an illusion, it has no power and we create more when we like and at the same time value it and de-value it on a whim, it isn't real, but our children are and our planet is?

Ironically, if we take the theme of money then it could easily be demonstrated that embracing new or ancient ways would in fact be very profitable if measured in money terms and we would also have the feel good factor of doing good. So who are against the change?

We have forgotten why we are playing the game and we can't seem to remember the rules and in order to compensate, we have created a new game that no one can ever win. It is time to change the game and bring the ultimate game back, it is our thoughts and actions that will change the world, not money in itself, but we can use it in a different way to a more positive end by remembering that we created the money and get it back into perspective and look at where the real value lies.

If you were in a desert dying of thirst what would you prefer, a wad of bank notes or some water? If you were diagnosed with a terminal illness would you prefer a healthy bank balance or a healthy body? If you were to lose a loved one could money compensate you?

What matters most is how we manage energy and it is all energy, after all we are energy beings and rely on energy for everything. We are bathed in the ultimate free energy every single day in the form of the sun. Nothing would exist at all without the sun. The adaptation and absorption of the sun's energy has made everything what it is today.

It took 300 million years to create fossil fuels and we release this stored energy in an instant by burning it for profit. Not only that, we are using up all the fossil fuels that the earth has stored and at an alarming rate. Again, plot the graph to obtain some scale and get it into perspective. It cannot continue, so are we being forced to act?

This is our "money" that is stored in our energy bank and we can use it properly and in different ways and all it takes, yes ALL it takes, is a subtle shift of mentality and we will see positive changes.

When did it all change? When did we become so materialistic? The bible states it started with Adam and Eve, others reckon it was when writing was introduced which started a focus on split-brain thinking rather than cohesive brain thoughts. Yet others believe it started with the concept of "ownership".

We may never know the real cause but we do know the issues involved now and we can stop it and rectify it and that is what this life and this experience is all about, learning and growing on our shared journey of discovery.

Why can we not open our eyes and see the reality before us?

I am reminded of an old gentleman I once knew, his name was Matthew. Matthew has since passed on but he was way ahead of his time when he lived on this plane, and although I didn't realise it at the time, I do now. Matthew introduced me to a new type of house construction using laminate and vacuum processing which was given lukewarm acceptance back then but would be very hot and topical now. He also had a solution that involved re-energising soil and treatment of waste using earthworm farms. I never grasped the concept then but I see it oh so clearly now.

No doubt there are millions of such examples throughout the world all waiting to be recognised and embraced. So what will initiate a change in the world? One way would be to inspire our children rather than make them fearful and restricted.

Getting back to children for a moment, if an alien visited earth for the first time and witnessed two births, one of a baby hippo and one of a child, who would it think was the most advanced? Would it be the hippo that is up walking and feeding itself within hours or the child that takes a year to learn how to walk? Fascinating when you consider how long we take to develop yet we continue to go on and surpass the hippo, but are we achieving all we can? I think not.

The level of materialism that we have achieved appears to have restricted the speed of our growth and once again as a result of shedding responsibility. Our children are capable of so much more if we would just create the environment that would stimulate and challenge them to imagine and experience rather than cosset, smother, and hide them away, poisoning their minds with fear to the extent that they are incapable of ever leading happy carefree lives.

Have we stopped caring about the most precious thing in life, our children? We appear to have, as our actions are about us and not them as we have fear of loss. How would we feel if something happened to them?

I sit and watch people bestow the virtues of a healthy life eating their Caesar salad and washing it down with bottled water whilst ordering burgers, chicken nuggets and fizzy drinks for their kids, once again teaching them the wrong way so that they can waste years of their lives later undoing it all.

Why can we not open our eyes and see the reality before us? We appear to be aliens on this planet, we don't seem to quite fit or belong, and we need so much extra stuff just to exist, clothes and so on. One would have thought that evolution would have done away with the need for clothes, shelter, heat, transport, even the pain of childbirth, but no, unlike others species, we don't quite fit.

Take the dolphins for example, totally at home in their own environment, an environment that covers two thirds of the planet's surface and is vastly unexplored. The dolphin is intelligent, has family units, communicates, learns not mimics, and obviously has desire and imagination as it masturbates.

Once again what species would an alien choose as the most advanced? We have created and become heavily reliant on technology and all creation is welcomed if used to a positive end, but we tend to use it to once again avoid responsibility, to distance ourselves and to make profit.

Weapons are a prime example as they make it all too easy for us to be lost in some virtual reality game. We really could press that button and kill thousands or millions if it ever escalates to a nuclear war. We have distanced ourselves from the reality of killing.

People are inherently good

This is a very important point as research has shown that we as human beings are not predisposed to killing. Studies involving man to man combat in wars interestingly show that only 2% of the combatants were actively engaged in killing. Some never fired their weapons and some fired to miss and some didn't even realise they were doing it and were subconsciously sabotaging their efforts.

Anyone who has used weapons will know that it only takes a fractional shift to be off target. The 2% that did engage were split into two camps, psychopaths who enjoyed the killing and didn't see it as wrong and those we would call warriors or heroes who recognised that killing was wrong but felt it served a purpose and regrettably, it had to be done.

So at a very deep level we don't want to kill our fellow man and if faced with it we would in the main choose to resist it. However, creating separation and distancing ourselves and shedding responsibility onto others, we allow it to take place. This should encourage us all to change and recognise that the world being portrayed as a bad place intent on killing is a myth when scaled and brought back into perspective.

Once again, those that have been fortunate to travel and experience the world will confirm that people are in fact inherently good but are manipulated and react out of fear in a negative fashion. It can all change as our basic programming for good already exists.

Technology helps by distancing oneself and making it easier to kill. The money required to fund this killing in the form of weapons is readily found in huge amounts fuelled by a misplaced fear and shedding of responsibility whilst struggling to look after the elderly or our children. Does that make sense to you? If not then why is it allowed to continue?

Unavoidable truths

Ironically, the self same advances in technology are showing us what we already knew. Why did we have to learn it all again? Are we caught in a Groundhog Day loop? All thought provoking stuff.

The key to the answer in my mind is that all that I say in this book is based on an unavoidable truth, and it may not be as eloquently put as it could be, or in as much detail as you would like, but the answer is that the reason that we seem out of place is that we are, we don't belong here, this is not our natural habitat.

In spiritual terms, we originally arrived on this planet as ethereal spiritual beings and regressed into the material world. We are an energy being, a spirit that inhabits a carbon body, a robot, whilst on this plane our purpose is to learn and experiment.

The robot, the carbon body has evolved along the way and we have allowed it to take too much control of our existence. Emotional chemicals have been created to enhance the experience, but lack of control over our thoughts have resulted in addictions and given even more control to the robot, our carbon shell.

We are seeing now that science is becoming the new spiritualists, they are seeing and proving what we really are and hopefully we will all be allowed to return to the reality that we once all knew and the regression will stop and we will start to progress. What were once poles apart are now merging into one, science, spiritualism and religion, and as stated before, leaving nowhere to hide for those in denial or those that choose not to open their eyes and see.

How many people have stated just before they passed over *I wish I had spent more time with my family and less at the office.* I can hear the counter arguments already, *yes I see that but once I complete this then I will take more time*, or *once I have X amount in the bank I will do this*. My brothers and a good friend Peter (Taz) immediately come to mind, I have heard them all say that. I have also watched a transformation in them all and all for different reasons.

Regardless, they are all very much aware that life could be better for us all, and all it takes is a change of thought.

Does this mean that it's ok to maim, kill and destroy our habitat and other species because it's a game or an illusion? NO! Absolutely not! We are here to learn and experience, we just need to remember why and get it all back into perspective and the message remains true whether you believe in the spiritual or the psychological aspect. It has the same impact and the same outcome if you learn to play the ultimate game.

It does not matter whether you look outwards or inwards, in every case you retain the power to create your own reality, you have been given the tools to do this in the form of imagination, and have the motivation through desire. The result is creation and our purpose is to experience this. Let me place this in order.

Desire, Imagination, Creation, Experience, is it an accident that this spells DICE? Obviously not as there is no such thing as an accident, it is validation for me that I have been given a glimpse of the truth and that I am starting to see the Universal picture. I have been given the DICE in order that I may start to play the game and I in turn have shared this with you.

In conclusion, we are all children of the Universe and we are all ageless and timeless immortals. At this juncture I would also like to highlight another area of separateness that has been created and that is the distance between man and woman.

We cannot on the one hand say we are all one and on the other look at women as second class. This is another area where ancient teachings have been distorted and politicised. How can anyone consider women as anything other than equal? Once again, regardless of spiritual or psychological viewpoints, empowering, embracing and accepting women globally as equal will rapidly put many of the world's wrongs right.

I would highly recommend that we also acknowledge the statement issued by Jackie Kennedy that the most important thing we can do in this life is bring children into the world and bring them up well. My prime motivation for starting this book was for my children, Clare and Scott, and in turn my Grandson Aidan, all of whom I love more than I will ever be able to adequately express in words. This expanded to those that I love and care for and who love and care for me, and as I wrote I realised it was for everyone who has been and yet to be.

The most receptive people to learn any game are without doubt children, they are like sponges, they soak up everything, however I am going to end this on a potentially controversial point and I smile as I write this. I was going to say teach your children well, but how can we do that when we are tainted and restricted ourselves?

Listen to children

The answer is to have courage, allow your children the freedom to explore, allow them to utilise their imagination to the full, don't restrict them, don't call them silly, don't ridicule them, explore the wonders of life with them. What are you scared of? Get them to share with you their dreams, their fantasies and place no boundaries on their possibilities.

Learn from your children, listen to them, play the game with them, allow yourself to enter their worlds and don't impose your world on them, see what they have to offer, you have nothing to lose and everything to gain, think about it.

Children's truth is laser-like and cuts through all the bullshit. Next time your child or any child makes you feel uncomfortable and you find yourself struggling with the answer to their questions or worse, lying to make life easier, STOP and dwell on the shift in energy that would take place by saying either that you don't know the answer to their question or you tell the truth as unpalatable as that may be.

JJ's son just so happens to be called Scot too but with one T. He could be classed as eccentric or unusual as he has a stimulating view of the world. When he learned to speak, one of the first things he said was that this world was much *badder* than he thought it would be before he came here. WOW!

There is an advert running in the USA just now where children ask, *can I have diabetes? Can I be obese? Can I cut my life short?* Our instinctive reaction is of course NO, but what do our actions say?

Children enter this world still in touch with the other world. Some can still see the astral world just as my grandson Aidan has demonstrated. In one way or another they all believe in magic, but do you?

You have the DICE

I sincerely hope that I have touched something in you, and if nothing else stimulated a constructive debate and a continuous search for the answers. I have not claimed to give the answers, just the rules to help you play this amazing game of life, and I have shared my own personal opinion with you.

I hope that I have opened your eyes to how and why everything works as it does and how we have a direct impact on the outcome.

There is a power in knowledge and a power in doing and whilst there have been a lot of words; the reality is that it is all quite simple and starts with a thought, a desire, that is shaped by the imagination. I hope that I have stimulated your imagination.

Play the game, play the ultimate game, and play the game of your life. You now have the rules so share this with your children and your children will show you the best way to play. You have already been given the DICE to start, Desire, Imagination Creation and Experience. It is your choice whether you positively resist the fear that is stopping you and create light in your life and in turn the world.

Play the game with love and do it with gratitude and when challenged by thought or circumstance, remind yourself that it is not in yours or anyone else's interests to play in fear. Just imagine for a moment what would happen if 6.5 billion people were all playing the game positively.

It's ultimately your choice, your game, your life. I have summarised everything in the next chapter *playing the game*, so read on and refresh your memory.

Cast your dice now and allow yourself to create light.

PLAYING THE GAME

Playing the Game

Purpose of the game	Creativity and Experience
Reward	To become Truly Rich
Minimum Number of Players	One – You
Maximum Number of Players	Unlimited
Number of Players Currently	World - approx 6.5 Billion
	Universe - Unknown
Requirements of Game	Yourself and your thoughts
Tools of the Game	Desire
	Imagination
	Creativity
	Experience
Essential Tips	Discipline and Responsibility
Referee	Karma
Length of Game	Eternity - with occasional short bursts of up to 100 years on the pitch

Number of levels	Multiple - with multiple dimensions and games in play at any one time
Obstacles	Free will, Fear, Time, and Other players

How to play

The purpose of the game is to create as much positive light as possible by fully emerging oneself in the game and interacting with as many other players as possible.

The time of play is irrelevant other than to gauge whether your intent in the game is true and consistent, what matters is experience as the more experience you obtain, the quicker you receive the required purity of light.

Everything starts with a Desire, a thought. This is at the root of all aspects of the game. The thought is shaped by the imagination and then created by intent and action, finally to become experience.

Every stage offers you the opportunity to resist and overturn the previous stage with either a negative or a positive.

Keep those initial thoughts pure and true of intent and the game becomes easy to play and you rise up the levels much sooner.

There have been a number of obstacles flung into the game to make it more challenging. You have the freewill to choose positive or negative, to receive abundance or reject it, to resist negative thoughts or embrace them.

Seeds of doubt are sown by fear, fear is one of the biggest challenges you will face.

Time has been created to ensure that your intent is true and to create a gap between the initial thought and the experience.

Others in the game will endeavour to influence your game.

You don't need to understand how the Universe works to play the game, you can still play by just trusting that it does, and see the results.

Scoring System

All positive resistance of negative thoughts and actions are rewarded by light, the more you are immersed in the game the more light you receive.

As you increase your light you move up the levels and once pure light is achieved you have reached the ultimate and can return to the source.

Purity is also obtained from assisting others in the game.

All negative thoughts and actions are reflected back at you and reduce light and your ability to rise to the next level.

Rules

The possibilities in the game are endless and are limited only by your imagination.

You can obtain guidance at any time by request from whatever source you choose through being open and aware, dreams, meditation, and so on.

Everything you desire can be created if you want it enough and focus upon it, however one should never try to influence, harm, or affect the free will of another in any way.

The game is all about creation not competition, everything should be about adding value and making things better for all.

There is no limit to how rich one can become as the Universe has abundance for all, what matters most is the intent and motivation behind the desire for the abundance.

It is important to know the difference between need and want.

Like will always be attracted to like, i.e. birds of a feather flock together, so to get what you want you must act and behave in that fashion and believe it.

Do unto others as you would have done unto you.

There is only now, nothing else, so act in the now, talk and think always in the present tense, I have, I am, etc.

You must give as you receive, not only are you helping others it shows that you have abundance, and like is attracted to like.

Be open to receiving, welcome all generosity.

Be grateful for all that you have. By being grateful you are demonstrating that you are playing the game properly.

Thoughts are treated like actions by the game and the Universe so a negative thought will negate a positive action and vice versa.

To be happy think happy thoughts, to be enthusiastic act enthusiastically, believing is seeing.

The irony is the lighter your spirit the easier it is to play the game.

The power is in the doing so the game must be experienced, every aspect of it, it cannot just be one thing, it has to be thought, action, sharing, most of all it must be fun and played with love.

EXERCISES

Exercises

I have decided that I will only give details on the actual exercises that I do personally and make reference to others so that you may seek them out yourself.

It should be noted that in every case you should do what feels right for you and take the time to look at various techniques and guidance as there is no absolute right way or best way, just what works for you. The sharing of what I do is purely to help you get started and then find your own way.

In all cases you must keep firmly in mind that a fundamental rule in all that you do is never to try and influence the free will of another and NEVER try to use these techniques or others to harm another as Karma will reflect it back at you.

I have listed below the various topics to be shared and I highly recommend that you take the time to read the book before reading or attempting any of the exercises so that you get the most from them.

Exercises

Happiness

Discipline and NOW

Responsibility and keeping your word

Focus and concentration

Know thy self

Dreams

Meditation

Asking for help

Setting the scene

Healing

Astral projection

Finances

Happiness

The ability to be happy is ironically one of easiest things you can do as it is purely a state of mind.

If you want to be happy think happy, think happy thoughts. Try it, bring into your mind a happy situation, you will start to feel happy just like the people that I ask to consider that they have 10 million in the bank.

When they actually bring that into their imagination you can see the smile start to appear. So it's a trick of the brain, just say *I am happy* and smile.

Build those neural networks and practice smiling, invoke the thoughts required to move the muscles to make you smile and smile and smile and be happy. Think those happy thoughts, it's fundamentally that simple.

Discipline

There are a few simple yet powerful themes running throughout this book and in turn life. One of the key ones is discipline. This may immediately turn people off or away and if this applies to you, you must look at yourself and ask why?

I have used the analogy of playing a game in the book as a lot of the requirements of playing a game equally apply to life. There are rules to be learned, if you want to get good at playing the game and get the most from it you require the discipline to both practice and apply the rules and it should be fun.

I catch myself many times thinking I should do this today but it's ok if I do it tomorrow.

NO, discipline yourself, you have made a promise to yourself to rearrange things so do what you have promised yourself as there is only NOW, tomorrow will bring you yet another set of excuses as to why you can put it off into the future and so it will continue.

I have explained in the book how you can make it easier, there is no need to for it to be hard, it's just a case of being self aware and using positive resistance to keep disciplined and do what you promised yourself.

Build new neural pathways that release pleasure every time that you positively resist something, remember 1% every day will grow exponentially and soon you won't recognise yourself.

There is only NOW all you have is NOW, the past has gone and is already being rewritten, the future is yet to come and when it does it will be NOW so its all you have, it's precious, it's a gift, hence the reason it's called the present.

So live in the NOW, live in the present, don't waste any more time, enjoy and embrace it all and don't send negative messages out to the Universe of *I want, I will try* etc.

In the NOW, *I am, I have*, live it, breathe it, believe it, know it, and you will see it, have the discipline to practice and take the time for you.

Responsibility

As far as you and the Universe and your reality is concerned there is only you, you create your own reality by the thoughts you have and the choices you make.

Just by accepting this, being aware of this, bringing it into your consciousness and taking and accepting full responsibility for it will transform your life.

You will as a matter of course stop judging, blaming or being disappointed by others and start to focus on taking responsibility for you. That's the best thing you can do for those you love.

Yes of course you can help others as long as that help is not just you offsetting responsibility for yourself by saying *oh look what I did for that person* etc., everything in your life is your responsibility, you chose it, accept that and if you don't like it make different choices.

What's stopping you? Mainly misplaced fear, and hopefully by reading the book a lot of that should be getting into perspective for you as the only fear you truly have is fear of fear itself and of taking responsibility for how great you truly are.

There is a Universe of infinite possibilities out there, by taking responsibility for your own life, basically the only thing that you can do as you cannot and should not take responsibility for anyone else.

I have kept the universal truth of simplicity running through the book and once again there is a very simple way you can start taking responsibility for yourself and that is by keeping your word.

Your word, your truth, can only be issued by you and can only be broken by you. To keep your word may sound simple but we all break it everyday, some in small ways, others in huge ways, it may be that you are late for a meeting and you say you had a puncture but in fact you slept in. Or you owe some money and you say you will pay when you get it whereas in fact you have used it for something else that you feel is more important.

All are breaches of your word and all will be played back to you in karma so the best way of starting to take responsibility is to be true of intent.

Do as you say, think and act in line with what you say and keep that promise to yourself and to others, keep your word and take responsibility for you and it will transform your life.

Focus and Concentration

I mentioned in the book how the sun beams billions of watts of energy in the form of sunlight onto us and yet with the simple act of putting a hat on or sun cream we can protect ourselves and yet if we focus a few watts of this energy into a laser we can cut diamonds and cure cancer.

The power of focus and concentration should never be underestimated. I was asked by many when I had the management consultancy practice what the key things to a successful business were and whilst I could list many ingredients that would all contribute towards a successful business, there was one key one that if missing would ensure failure and that was focus.

We will all have experienced the increase in ability when we achieve that focused or concentrative sate commonly known as "in the zone" where everything just falls into place.

Whilst focused, you also obliterate the clutter and noise around you and you give a clear message with your concentrated mind.

Fortunately we can practice and train our minds to concentrate and stay focussed.

Try a couple of simple exercises and then build up to the point where you can influence your surroundings

I am going to use the number eight a lot in this and this is no accident, numbers feature a great deal in universal laws particularly around the range 6-8.

Digressing slightly, 3 and 7 are the most popular numbers in the world and the number 8 is held as being a very lucky number in the East.

In business I learned that when pricing contracts, i.e. submitting tenders, I should expect to win 1 in every six or seven if my pricing was accurate, less than this I was too expensive, more than that I was too cheap. Over the years this proved accurate and helped me with forecasts and planning.

When teaching or training a group of people, if you have less than 8 you will advance in line with the quickest and if more than 8 you will be in line with the slowest and so it goes on.

Exercises

When practicing focus and concentration it goes without saying that it is best tackled somewhere where you will not be disturbed.

In this case count backwards from 100 to 1 eight times, until you can do it with no mistakes and each time you make a mistake do it again.

Then count 100 downwards using even numbers eight times, likewise with odd numbers, and lastly reducing by three each time, it might sound easy, try it.

Next find an object and study it solidly for say three minutes. If you can, do eight minutes. Close your eyes and picture the object, turn it around in your head and see it from every angle, keep doing this until you get it 100% accurate each time.

To move to the next level you need to involve other senses like taste, smell and touch so choose an object that best invokes these aspects. Study it for as long as it takes and then close your eyes and bring it to life in your imagination.

Exercises

Having achieved that successfully each time with objects of your choice you can then create events and scenarios in your mind, remembering that the brain knows no difference between what you see and imagine.

We are all pretty adept at this when it comes to sexual fantasy which proves you can do it, now you can increase your scope.

Why would you do this? Well now you can more accurately manifest into your life what you truly want by seeing how you feel by having it.

It may be when you go through all of this you actually realise that it's not what you want and that has saved you a great deal of time and energy, if it is what you want then you can more accurately and powerfully bring it into your life.

For all those amongst you that are put off by the above for whatever reason you can start to create what you want by first doing your own My Reality Sheet - a few short paragraphs highlighting what you want your reality to be. Then find pictures that represent your reality and put a picture of yourself in the middle and start building up your dream collage, your reality.

Ideally keep this in a folder, keep it private, it's yours and yours only, don't let anyone's negative energy tarnish your dream.

Start to write down your dream and in each case describe it in as much detail as you can. What it will look like, why you want it, how it will improve your life etc., and as you do this you will automatically find what you really want from a fleeting desire.

There is a magic in writing it down, you are giving it energy by doing so, and you are practicing focus and concentration in a way you are comfortable with, it will achieve the same results.

The only difference with doing it in your head is you can do it anywhere at anytime.

Know Thy Self

I have purposely placed this in the middle as it is something that you can start immediately but equally it could take a lifetime. Regardless, it is important that you take the time to understand you.

You can reflect on this at any time but it's also worth taking the time and writing down every event that caused you to feel the emotions listed below and ask yourself honestly what the outcome was.

Having done so, forgive yourself, acknowledge the lesson, put it aside and let it go and get on with your life as everything can be fixed and everything is going to be ok

Take some time every day to make sure you have your thinking right.

Learn to recognise those moments when your intention is not as pure as it should be, when your actions are not in line with your intent.

Ask yourself why you are doing, thinking, saying something and what you are going to get out of it? Is it adding value?

Ask yourself what karmic debt might arise from your particular actions. Is it worth it?

Whenever you feel a negative thought coming through, look at it, what is it really about? Resist the temptation to fall victim to it, learn to adopt an objective approach to these thoughts, they have come for a reason, if you don't find out the cause then you are going to come across them again and again and again until you get to the root of them and can banish them forever.

You need to be brutally honest with yourself.

Put simply, are you acting or reacting, is it positive or negative? Pro activity (positive actions) comes from a loving space and they are taking you closer to where you have chosen to go.

Reactivity is coming from a fear filled negative space where you are trying to avoid something and run away from it, you are not choosing any direction other than away from the issue, positively resist this.

This and this alone is enough, but if you wish to delve deeper you can by writing down each time you recall feeling any of the following and what the outcome was.

You don't need to do this as it could be reinforcing it but some may want to in order to obtain clarity and to reduce the risk of coming across them again.

These are just a few examples of traits and as you get to know yourself, you will be able to add some of your own.

Exercises

Positive Traits

Love

Purity of thought

Generosity

Compassion

Kindness

Feeling complete

Forgiveness

Gratitude

Empathy

Acceptance

Honesty

Negative Traits

Hatred

Guilt

Greed

Resentment

Selfishness

Feelings of inadequacy

Vengefulness

Jealousy

Pity

Denial

Dishonesty

Are you being kind to your self? Remember that whatever you do now, will most certainly have an impact on YOU, the effect is instant in other realms but may take some time to be felt by you on this earthly plane.

Be honest with yourself. This is very important but you would be shocked at how many people are simply not honest and dupe themselves into thinking that things are not the way they really are.

You are creating your very own reality, remember this, if you indulge in negative thinking or wish ill will on anyone else, then you are going to pay for this one way or another. You must learn to banish these negative thoughts and train yourself to allow only the purest of thoughts and intentions to come through.

If you attach too much importance to material possessions and money, if you compare yourself to others and find yourself wishing you had what they had or worse, if you feel resentment because they have something that you don't, then you are undoing all the positive thinking you have done in one mental flash. Stop it, learn to control your ego, and learn to humble yourself.

You are what you think, what you eat, what you say, what you do, you are your own manifestation and your own creation. The Universe doesn't discriminate, only people do.

Learn from other people. If you encounter someone who seems to have more than their fair share of personal disasters and misery, in whatever form, you can learn from that. What is it about their thinking, their actions or what they portray that could have resulted in such despair?

Likewise do the same with those that have a great life.

Dreams

I have spoken at length in the book about the importance of dreams and there is little more I wish to add here other than to recommend a book called 24 hour dream breakthrough, I got a lot from it.

However once again keeping it simple, you can do the following before going to sleep. Ask yourself a question that you want an answer to, be as clear and as simple as you can in the question, your answer will reflect your question and complex questions will get complex answers.

Keep a pad and pencil next to your bed or a tape recorder, or use the notes section at the back of this book and write down or record what comes into your mind and do it as soon as you wake up as it will start to fade very quickly.

There is another book I would like to recommend called Practical Intuition by Laura Day, this will help you decide what it is you need and in turn want and help you tune in during your waking time.

Meditation

Before starting this, a word of warning, this is powerful and not to be taken lightly and should be treated with respect. It works if you do it with love and an open heart and mind. Never ever try to use it to harm anyone or with selfish intent or it will come back to you.

Find a quite place where you are unlikely to be disturbed for approx half an hour. If possible, light a candle as it sets the scene and shows that you are starting something special.

If you want to go the whole hog and mirror what I do, take four candles, draw an imaginary circle, place one candle at the south, one at the north, one at east, and one in the west point, and sit in the middle. This also represents the four main elements. Not easy to do unless you have your own space undisturbed. Then visualise three circles of light being drawn around you, for some reason in my case these always become golden and start to rise and fall rhythmically, and ask for protection, ask that nothing negative is able to cross these lines.

Sit comfortably and as erect as possible i.e. straight back and neck with loose clothing on and place one hand on your forehead, the other on the back of your head at the nape of your neck.

Breathe in through your nose from the stomach and out through the mouth. Repeat until you are relaxed. Ninety eight percent of people breathe badly, they breathe through the chest. It is a proven fact that by learning to breathe through the abdomen you relax, lower blood pressure, and increase energy. There are many books or articles on this subject if you want to research further.

Having done this, place your hands in a relaxed meditative position, imagine a white soft healing light surrounding your whole body and each time you breathe in that light enters your body, imagine it filling your whole body and as you breathe out, breathe out all negative energy.

Once the light has filled your body you can start to go into meditative mode.

Imagine any situation or person or whatever that fills you with pure love and allow that to lift your spirits to new highs.

Repeat in your head a special word of your choice that helps you keep the feeling of absolute love (you will instinctively know what to use) if you like, a mantra, that if you said it out loud you would feel it vibrate in your head. There are many books and articles on mantras.

Once again the next bit is optional.

Focus on the middle of your forehead jut above your nose (pineal gland or third eye) you will at some point feel it vibrate, you know then you are in tune. Imagine that you have reached up through the top of your spine through your head to touch the stars, imagine drawing energy from there down into your body, and centre it just below your rib cage, approx three fingers below. Then imagine that you can, like the roots of trees, reach down through the earth and draw energy from there and centre it. You are now drawing your power and energy from the Universe or the Divine power or the Great Spirit what ever feels right for you. Feel all the energy from the earth, rocks trees, sea, sky, fire, etc., all are available to you. Allow it to flow, to surge through you, and send it back as love and light to everyone. I visualise all my chakras opening up as I draw the light through my body, I also reinforce that I am at one and peace with everything with my little enchantments

If you are doing the mediation purely for you then allow whatever thoughts come into your head to come in and just let them go, don't hold onto anything, just feel energised and full of love and ask for guidance and strength to trust.

Continue like this for as long as possible, but ideally around 20 minutes or so. Before finishing make sure that you are still filled with light and love, if not re-energise by imagining yourself being filled again, just filling yourself with thoughts of love will draw the energy in.

Allow it to flow through you rather than hold on to it. Then before finishing breathe good energy into your body through your nose, deep into you, then with an open mouth expel with some vigour until you are totally empty of all the negative energy in your body and repeat this negative energy expulsion four times.

Thank all those that have helped you in your mind and then tell yourself that you are coming out of that state and that you wish the feeling of love and energy to stay with you all day, and then very, very slowly open your eyes as if it were like the sun rising over the horizon.

I, where possible, endeavour to meditate twice a day however I accept that my travel schedule and finding suitable places does have an impact on this but I never let that stress me and just look forward to when I can meditate.

Asking for help

There are a number of ways to ask for help. You can ask just before you go to sleep for an answer or guidance and you can also ask when you are meditating.

We can split this into three distinct areas:

1. Asking for general guidance

2. Asking your spirit guide

3. Asking a specific person

1. Asking for general guidance

General Guidance is straight forward and the only effort you need to make, just like asking in your dreams, is to formulate the question as accurately as possible before starting to meditate and then when in a fully meditative state ask the question and be open to whatever transpires.

2. Asking your spirit guide

Asking for help from your spirit guide or your guardian angel is when you ask the person watching over you or whatever label you wish to place on them, they don't care what you call them. It is them that pop that little thought into your head to stop for a drink and suddenly you meet someone you have not seen for years or who tell you to strike up a conversation with a stranger when you otherwise would not.

When in your meditative state imagine the most tranquil and if you like sacred or magical place you can, basically anything that gets you into the correct frame or state of mind. Raise your spirit as high as you can, be as carefree and happy as you can, be as grateful as you can and ask that your guide come to you, open your arms to the possibility, welcome them in.

You will either see something in your minds eye (don't force it or fight it, let it come) or you will feel their presence, once again don't fight it or force it and never be disappointed if you don't see or feel anything, just keep doing it and ask the question regardless and be open for an answer.

3. Asking a specific person

Asking a specific person for help can be asking them to assist you or even to leave your life or perhaps to do something in particular, in every case you cannot force or expect anyone to do anything against their will.

Once in a meditative state ask the person to come to you and ask if you can make contact with them. You can do this by imagining a silver light chord connecting you with them and this can either be from your pineal gland or heart chakra.

Once they come to you either you picture it or feel it, imagine or picture you bathing them in light and doing it with complete love and affection, no bad intent. Actively bathe them in light 8 times and then ask your question.

If you wish the person to leave your life for whatever reason, visualise them in the palm of your hand as you bathe them in light and when finished gently blow them from your palm as you thank them for bringing the awareness of the problem or problems to you and that you have learned your lesson and it is time to move on and that you wish them every success and happiness.

Setting the Scene

If you are attending a meeting or any event that you wish to go smoothly you can also bathe that in light as above but as it will involve others, all you can ask for is that it runs as smoothly as it should and that the outcome be the best for all concerned.

Astral projection

I have experienced astral projection as stated in the book and for those who are interested I would recommend the book "Journey out of the body" by Robert A. Munro.

Healing

Everything starts with thoughts so your health etc. is all influenced by thought. In turn thought is an energy vibration and anything that can influence the thought can influence your health so first and foremost have healthy positive thoughts.

Healing can come in many forms and conventional medicine now looks to what is termed alternative but what should be termed original.

There are many forms of vibration related healing, from colour to sound, acupuncture and so on. I have tried most of the well known types in an experimental fashion including a machine that can read your vibrations and tell you what's wrong or what is missing from your body. At the time I experienced this there were only four of these machines in the UK so this type of healing is still in a very early stage. I expect we will be seeing more of this in the future.

When it comes to remote healing something that I have done successfully before, you should do the following.

Once again ask to connect with whoever it is you want to help and bathe them in light, but instead of asking a question state that you want them to heal.

In serious cases i.e. those who have terminal illnesses, you acknowledge that if it is their time then you ask for their passing to be as pain free as possible and free from trauma.

You also say if it is not their time to pass then you seek help to heal them. You imagine them bathed in light and you say that their illness, cancer cells or whatever, have now served their purpose in this dimension, and they can now move on and be grateful for all the help you have been given.

Picture the person in perfect health. That is how you want to see them NOW, to be free from pain and illness.

Focus on that for as long as you feel comfortable doing it.

Abundance

Abundance is having more than you need. I have described above the steps to have mental and spiritual abundance however to be Truly Rich one should have abundance in everything. It is everyone's right as there are endless possibilities and this includes material wealth and financial abundance providing of course that you have it in perspective and you control it and not the other way around.

I have described above how you can bring your dreams into reality, this will include financial but its worth mentioning a couple of extra things.

Living in the now means that you believe now that you are already rich, wealthy and you act accordingly, you do not attach worry to paying bills as you know you will comfortably be able to pay those bills.

You show that you are comfortable with money by always having cash on you, as much as you can sensibly carry around with you, as like attracts like.

Savings can also be an issue if they are from a worry or a negative perspective i.e. saving for a rainy day etc. as that is wishing that scenario upon you.

There is a difference between saving cash for you for a special occasion such as a holiday and saving for the sake of hoarding.

Create a magic envelope and put a minimum of ten percent of any money you have coming in into it each time and watch it grow so that when the holiday or special purchase comes along it's as if you got it for free.

Also in order to receive you need to give, it shows that you have abundance and are grateful and that you care about others.

The more you give the more you will receive, never give conditionally always give unconditionally, that way your intent is pure.

Never give anything that you cannot afford as again it will tarnish your intent but give freely and frequently and it will flow back to you especially if you are open to receiving.

Be grateful for everything and anything, the Universe does not understand money it's a man made thing given power only by man so the Universe does not see the difference between 2 coins and 2 million so always be conscious of that.

Let's take a simple example. You are out for a meal with friends and you say you will treat everyone. Is that because you genuinely wish to treat them or to show off, or is it expected of you?

Likewise if someone offers to treat you, accept it graciously if you think it's from the heart, if you think they can't afford to share it and if you think they are doing so with the wrong intent take control as you see fit.

Do it in your own way, do it to make a difference, do it from the heart, and do it knowing that there is abundance and infinite possibilities in the Universe.

I hope that you do these exercises as I know it will transform your life and you will help many others, without them ever knowing it was you, which is the best way.

Remember never do anything with any ill will or to try and force your will on others, it will only backfire, only ask for what is right for them. If you can learn to conduct all that you do in life with an open heart and mind what a magical person you will be then.

You were destined to shine, don't fight it anymore.

A new beginning awaits you...

Notes

Notes

Notes

Please visit www.widerhorizons.co.uk for more information on how you could be rewarded for reading and recommending this book.